CLEAR SPACE

How to Make Room for What Matters Most
in Your Home & Life

Smith Banfield

BALBOA.PRESS
A DIVISION OF HAY HOUSE

Balboa Press books may be ordered through booksellers or by contacting:

Balboa Press
A Division of Hay House
1663 Liberty Drive
Bloomington, IN 47403
www.balboapress.com
1 (877) 407-4847

Author Photo by Alyssa Peek
Cover Image by Smith Banfield

Print information available on the last page.

ISBN: 978-1-9822-4248-0 (sc)
ISBN: 978-1-9822-4250-3 (hc)
ISBN: 978-1-9822-4249-7 (e)

Library of Congress Control Number: 2020902191

Balboa Press rev. date: 03/23/2020

To my husband, Ross.
Everything is possible.
143

CONTENTS

INTRODUCTION

Here's a secret: Being organized is the *path*, not the destination.

Let me back up for a minute.

Given the title of this book, I'm sure you already have an inkling that I'm going to share my proven method for decluttering and organizing your home. And I will. Perhaps you are hoping that my system will be *the* system that finally brings order into your life. By following a bunch of strict rules, you will, at last, know what to do and never have to frantically search for your misplaced car keys again.

Over the past eight years, I've helped countless people transform their relationships with their stuff and, in that process, transform their homes. But it wasn't by imposing an inflexible regimen. Other people's rules don't work. What *does* work, I've learned, is curiosity. I teach people how to be inquisitive and non-judgmental about why they have what they have, and also to observe how most of what they have is preventing them from living the lives they truly want.

That's where the real magic happens.

I know this to be true, not just from my work with my clients, but because I've lived it myself.

You see, I wasn't born organized. I was a mess, always wrestling with my precious things. For a long time. A really long time. People who are overwhelmed by their lives and their belongings already feel like failures; their self-talk is soul-crushing. It was for me. But one fateful day (and I promise I'll tell you the whole story later), I lost all of my stuff.

Literally. All of it. (Except for my beloved Tigger!)

Taking a crash course to learn who I was - and who I might be - without my stuff to hide behind, I had to get curious real fast. And a funny thing happened once I did: I discovered that I wasn't defined by what I owned.

You aren't either.

That's why I know I can help those of you who have struggled to create order in your homes. If I could become organized, and now build a successful business helping others become organized, you can, too. I am confident that by sharing my approach, you will also have success.

This book is divided into two parts: WHY and HOW.

While you may be tempted to skip to the second half where I show you how to take action, it is the process of questions in the first half of the book which will create the foundation to help you take purposeful and sustainable action in the second half.

Please don't skip ahead. (*Please.*)

I've learned in my work that many people don't take the time to gently question themselves about their belongings. They don't understand why they have what they have, or where it came from, so they get confused about where exactly it should go in their homes or why it's there in the first place. More importantly, they aren't clear on who they are today and whether their stuff actually embodies that. Instead, most people live with things that reflect some version of who someone else expected them to be or told them who they were.

That's the source of all clutter.

Once you're clear about that, then it's time to get to work.

The second half of the book is the nuts and bolts of HOW to do that work. I will guide you through the steps I use with my clients and in my own home. I've laid out these steps so you can take on your entire home because I've found this is the best way to understand all that you own.

Yes, it's a big job.

But you will only have to do it once.

If you're reading this book, you're done with band-aid fixes.

To truly create change in your space, you have to be willing to roll up your sleeves and do some heavy lifting. It may feel overwhelming at times but - and this is an important *but* - you *have to* be kind to yourself. This is my only hard and fast rule (well, there's one more but we'll get to that later).

So, take a deep breath and get ready to learn about yourself.

My greatest hope for this book is that it provides you many lightbulb moments that result in a clear space that functions in harmony with your every need. If that doesn't feel possible for you, start by softly introducing this new belief: I believe it is possible for me to become organized.

Right now, that's all you need to begin.

That's enough.

WHY

1

STUFF ISN'T LOVE

So here it is, the big question:

HOW DOES YOUR STUFF MAKE YOU FEEL?

Your first thought might be "What business is that of yours? I'm just here to deal with my clutter, thank you very much."

One kind of person says:

"I love my stuff. It makes me feel safe and secure. I have lots of it. And I wade through it every day. Every time I move a pile, I'm reminded of how protected I am. This stack of magazines from 1998 makes a perfectly good snack table as I Netflix and chill. And the dirty clothes on the floor keep my feet nice and warm, so . . . I'm good."

That person would not pick up this book. That person is perfectly fine with their clutter. And that's great! I'm not looking to change that person. But that's not you. You're here because you've struggled for far too long with the feeling of being overwhelmed by your belongings. You're here because you're ready for a lasting solution and are tired of quick fixes that don't work. You're here because you're exhausted by justifying all of your stuff and how much of it you have.

You're here because you want a simpler life.

So do I.

I'm not here to point the finger at those of us who have accumulated too much stuff. My home isn't perfect, either. There are times when I'm caught up helping my clients and, by the end of the week, I have piles of stuff around the house.

Just like you.

But because I've studied my household's habits, and created systems and solutions to manage my stuff, it's simple to get my home back in order. And the confidence I have in knowing where everything belongs brings me ease.

By following the guidelines in this book, you'll get there too.

I want to shine as much light as possible on the many ways stuff comes into our lives and takes over. While our shopping habits are the obvious source of much of it, let's look elsewhere. There's the daily stream of mail. We're surrounded by other people giving us material objects whether with the kindness of a gift or something as irresistible as a free sample. Most important of all is how our own vulnerability, which is often overlooked, isn't acknowledged. By understanding all of the various avenues by which things arrive, we can strategize ways of closing these avenues off or at least slow down the rate at which things enter our lives.

We're in a crisis of abundance.

Without our realizing it, the speed and ease with which we accumulate stuff, has never been higher and has resulted in an actual abundance problem. Somewhere along the way, we were taught to buy our happiness and avoid our feelings. The same folks who are overwhelmed by their belongings are still searching for that one perfect thing to obtain that will finally make them feel better once and for all.

This isn't a coincidence. It's near impossible to avoid or resist.

Advertising, credit cards and convenience bewitch you. Collectively, they've cast their spell. Their seductions are everywhere promising that your life will somehow improve if you only have more stuff. Come over here where the grass is greener and the air is cleaner. You'll look cool in these sneakers. You'll tame your busy life with this new pocket planner. Happiness guaranteed! There you are surrounded by a pile of crap and they've got your money. It's a perfect system. For *them*.

Have you ever noticed that anything you search for online or talk about near your phone instantly ends up in your Instagram feed and pop-up ads? Amazon reminds you of things you looked for, and a company that you never heard of emails you with offers of free shipping. As potential consumers, we are stalked until we finally click and purchase.

Like many of you, I was raised to save up for something I really wanted; however, that isn't how the world operates anymore. This quaint notion has gone by the wayside. Buy now. Figure out how to pay for it later. As of December 2019, the total outstanding US Consumer Debt was almost $14 trillion. (Trillion?! Do you get that? I had to look up how many zeroes that is: $14,000,000,000,000. That's absurd!) Is it any wonder our belongings are overwhelming us?

Paying with credit cards has become the norm. We've gone from wondering what I can get with the twenty-dollar bill I have in my wallet - having to make a conscious choice about handing over the cash - to having a pile of clothes that I want to buy; here's my card, and I'll worry about if I can afford it when I get the bill. Accordingly, average Americans now hold fifty-two percent more debt than they did ten years ago.

Which isn't surprising.

It has never been easier for us to buy things. Convenience is only a click away. The internet has transformed not only what and how much we can access, but where we can access it from, and how quickly we can get it as well.

Smartphones are the equivalent of carrying around a shopping mall in your pocket. How many times have we added items to an online cart in order to get the free shipping? Or how many impulse purchases we make because of the email we received? "You are such a special customer, you can save 30% right now on something you don't even need, but don't delay or YOU WILL MISS OUT." It's so easy. *Too easy.* There's never a moment to stop and consider what, why or how we are purchasing our stuff. If by chance we do question a purchase, we're quick to justify or explain it away.

After all, we deserve it! I feel stuck in my job. I feel stuck in my relationship. I feel stuck in my home. The quick fix of stuff provides immediate comfort. I feel powerless over these problems in my life so I will distract myself from my misery. We numb ourselves with bright and shiny objects that lose their luster the second they are purchased. We make these objects so meaningful that we keep inviting them into our homes, telling ourselves stories about who we'll be once we own this stuff. There we are, our latest desire in our hands, and then what? The thrill is over. Here I am, surrounded by new treasures. Shouldn't I feel like I'm safe and secure and loved? Before we know it, we're back to the same old us, further trapped by more stuff.

We don't need to suffer through this escalating cycle. We don't have to stay trapped and overwhelmed.

The spell can be broken.

We can open up clear space in our homes, our minds and in our lives.

I'm here to help.

Believe me, I've seen it all. (Like the time I discovered the mummified family cat in a garbage bag behind some boxes on a shelf in the basement.) What I've learned is that we'll never begin to solve our stuff problem until we face our vulnerability and realize that stuff isn't a substitute for love.

VULNERABILITY & EMOTIONS

Much of the clutter in our lives is invisible and unquestioned. The piles of mail, bags filled with purchases and guilt that gets hidden in the closet, the bottomless pit of a purse, stuffed with anything that comes across our paths to deal with "later" or the dining room table where we put things "just for now" all become too much to process so, instead, we ignore it.

Until we can't.

Awareness hits us that we have too much stuff. Something needs to change. But how? We want to fix this mess quickly and pretend it never happened. But we have no idea where to begin or which steps to take. We're left feeling embarrassed and paralyzed.

In that moment of discomfort, I've witnessed people respond in two ways:

1. **Denial:** pretend that EVERYTHING'S FINE, forging a new pathway through piles in the shrinking hallway, as they slowly drown in the rising tide of their belongings.
2. **Reactive:** try to organize quickly and randomly, as they shove yet more things into bursting closets and drawers only to feel defeated and worse.

Here's a different and more powerful option: Transform that moment of discomfort into an opportunity to genuinely stop and think about how much of our lives are unintentionally being controlled by the inanimate objects in our home and the emotional and subconscious negative relationship we have to them.

Which is scary.

This is as it should be.

Let's look at the amygdala, sometimes referred to as our "lizard brain", the part of our brain stem which is programmed to react in fear. This most primitive part of our brain perceives any change, or possible change, as a threat to our survival and labels that change as a danger. All kinds of fears and judgments rush in.

Relationship-based fears feel like "Something horrible will happen to me if I get rid of the blouse Aunt Mary gave me, which never fit, and I'm ungrateful for wanting to let go of it and I will hurt her feelings".

Lack-based fears show up as "I paid good money for that state-of-the-art juicer I never used which I bought two years ago for my new diet. Getting rid of it means I'll always be overweight and, therefore, unloved."

Status-based fears take hold as "Even though my current phone works just fine, and I have two old ones in a drawer, I need to have the latest model so I am seen as successful and in charge and not the impostor I know myself to be."

Identity-based fears sound like "If I let go of my county basketball trophies and track medals from junior year, I will forget that happy time of accomplishment and I will never achieve anything great in my life again and prove, once and for all, that I am a loser."

Multiply these fears by all of the items currently in your home.

Of course you're afraid!

Loaded with so much meaning, power and emotions, these things are no longer individual items. It makes sense to feel frightened because this is how your stuff holds you hostage. I want to remind you to pause and stay open in this moment of fear and know that it's natural and universal for these objects to have such a stronghold over our lives. We're all so deeply embedded with the fear of not being enough or having enough, we deeply believe we don't have enough, even as we are being suffocated by our belongings. Our work together is to understand what it means for you to have enough, and more powerfully, to truly believe that you are enough. You don't need so much stuff to prove it.

STUFF IS NOT LOVE

No matter what, your stuff will never love you back. Take a moment to think about that. When was the last time your overstuffed cosmetics drawer made you feel good about yourself? Do your "skinny" clothes help you love and accept yourself just the way you are? I'm guessing they don't make you feel very good at all. Those powerful and repetitive thoughts about "not-enoughness" are lingering, insisting on taking up precious physical and mental space. When you consciously clear your space and invite new and positive energy in, you allow actual love into your life.

Once we accept the beliefs that we've attached to all of our stuff, we're afraid to let them go because these beliefs give us a false sense of reassurance that we're okay. We're like the child hiding under a security blanket to make sure the monsters under the bed can't get him.

But I'm here to tell you, you already are okay, and you don't need your stuff to verify it. Let me say it again (and I promise it won't be the last time), stuff isn't love and your worth is not measured by your stuff.

Once our eyes are open, and we've awakened from the spell, we see for the first time that we have imprisoned ourselves to a life-sentence with our stuff. The cell block door opens easily since we've possessed the key the whole time. We just need to open the lock, let ourselves out, and start walking.

BUILDING AWARENESS

So how do we begin?

With awareness.

It's the essential tool to break the cycle of being engulfed by our belongings. Whether you're buried by clothing, food, papers, or whatever version chaos takes on for you, we can learn to study ourselves without judgment. We start to learn who we are, and how, and why we bring stuff into our lives. Empowered by this knowledge, we can break the trance.

We'll learn to ask questions like: Is this really my taste? What am I drawn to? Will this purchase make me feel better or worse ten steps down the road? Am I just trying to soothe myself? We learn to decipher the difference between shopping for necessity and shopping to distract ourselves from our feelings. When we find ourselves browsing store aisles or the internet mindlessly, this is when we will start to ask: What am I feeling? Do I really need anything? Is it wise to bring more stuff into my space? What will I let go of to make room for this?

In my experience, I've learned that all of the answers to these questions show up in three areas of awareness. We'll be looking at these in much greater detail moving forward in the book, but, just so you know where we're headed, let's take a moment to look at them more broadly:

1. **We evolve. Things do not.**
    I can look back at photos of myself, from ten, twenty and even thirty years ago and remember how much I loved that dress, or car, or piece of furniture. But I also know that these things I used to love wouldn't fit in my life today, because I can also clearly see that I'm not who I was then. It's possible to have short love affairs with our stuff but, in the moment of bringing objects into our lives, we don't see that they are ephemeral

and have their own lifecycle. When I work with clients, I see how things that they thought were permanent are, in fact, merely temporary. Those items are usually the ones at the bottom of some pile, hidden by the newest acquisitions. Sifting through the pile is like studying the rings of a tree trunk, each layer revealing the passage of time. With the tool of awareness, we will acknowledge the reality that our lives are constantly evolving and changing since we are personally evolving and changing all of the time. Our objects and the solutions to store them also need to evolve and change, working with us instead of against us.

2. **We are not our stuff.**

   Freed by embracing the reality of our ever-expanding, ever-growing lives, we can release our habitual hold on items because we see they only represented an idea of who we were, or who others expected us to be. We see how these items keep us stuck in place. Now that we understand we are not defined by our physical objects, we can face and clear out our past to make room for our future. We can create space in which we can fully stretch out our arms wide open and invite freedom into our lives. This awareness that we are not our stuff offers another kind of liberation. We can ask ourselves this question: Who is my stuff for? Does my stuff serve my fulfillment and ease, or does it bolster my identity in the eyes of others? (Remember: Stuff isn't love.)

3. **With objects, comes responsibility.**

   If a child wants a dog, a parent first talks to them about the responsibility of caring for an animal and everything that responsibility encompasses. For the dog to thrive, the child commits to feeding the dog, walking the dog, and cleaning up its messes, even on the days it's raining or when the child doesn't want to get out of bed. The reward, of course, is unconditional love and a faithful friend. What if we looked at the things we bring into our lives through the lens of that kind of responsibility? Could we make a similar commitment to caring for ourselves by accepting the responsibility of our stuff? This shift in awareness is as transformative as it is unconsidered. Some of these responsibilities we honor already, such as changing the oil in our car or checking the air pressure of our tires in order to drive safely and extend the life of this substantial investment we've made. What if we looked at all the clothing in our closet this way? Or considered the uninvited responsibility of the plastic-wrapped plastic cutlery that comes with your take-out dinner delivery which you don't use because you are eating at home anyway? Once it's in your hand, you've taken ownership. It's become your responsibility. Do you throw it away or jam it in the drawer with the other ten packets of plastic-wrapped plastic cutlery? No matter what you decide to do about that spork, it will eventually end up as garbage. And where does that end up? Most likely in the ocean with countless other knives and forks. I'm not trying to intimidate you with this example. Instead, I want to give you permission to refuse these kinds of unwanted responsibilities. I mean, how many things do you want to be responsible for in life? You've got enough on your plate already.

Building awareness is the key to freedom and the goal of this book. As I said at the start of this chapter, I am not here to shame, blame or judge you about the stuff in your home and how it affects your life. We were all raised by people who didn't have the dizzying array of choices and ease of acquiring stuff the way we do now. Our ease of consumption is unprecedented in human history. We haven't caught up mentally or spiritually with this transformation yet.

My job is not to preach or burden you with perfection either. There is no perfection, no exact number of items you should own or remove from your life. What I'm interested in is seeing you surrounded by things you love and things you use, and forgiving yourself for spending too much money on that cashmere sweater that wasn't flattering ever. Let someone else love that sweater and be thrilled that they got such a great bargain at the consignment shop.

Once we become aware of how our lives can be controlled by our belongings, the effects are monumental. You'll never look at your stuff in the same way again. The panicked feeling to hold onto everything will dissolve. You can finally relax and breathe again, believing you will be provided with what you need when you need it.

Release the feelings of shame, guilt, and scrutiny. There is no place for it here. Besides, they will only slow you down. My wish for you, in offering this information, is one of clarity and curiosity. When we can truly see who we are now, rather than who we used to be, we can consciously clear space for all of the possibilities of who we may become in the future. We create the space for real love and connection in our lives.

So ... what's the deal with all your stuff? Why is it there? How did you end up with all of it? How does it make you feel? Please remember to be kind to yourself with your answers. We are searching for information, not looking for another way to feel bad about yourself. There isn't one right way to live in your space. I find that so many of my clients are trying to live by someone else's rules and goals, rules and goals that don't even line up with who they really are or how they want to live.

Sometimes I think they have forgotten who they are.

But this is a beautiful starting point. I invite them, like I'm inviting you now, to claim their space and step into a new way of being.

2

BECOMING AWARE

HOW DO I BEGIN?

Let's start with this question:

Who are you today?

Take a moment and really think about it. This is not a time to consider who other people think or expect you to be, or even who you expected yourself to be. Quiet all the other voices and simply tune into you.

Just you. Today.

Don't be scared, you're okay. Whatever your answer is, you're good. You're discovering what lights you up, what brings excitement, pleasure and beauty into your life. Expect this to be fun and feel good.

As I work with my clients, I see time and again that people who are unclear around that question, live in spaces that are also unclear.

When it comes to creating a functional space, it is imperative to have information about yourself because it's how you will discover *why* you have what you have. With an objective eye, you'll begin to truly see your space and your stuff, their value and how they help or hinder your world. Then you can make informed decisions that keep you on track and clutter-free rather than distracted and overwhelmed.

An easy place to get started is with a design quiz. Rediscover the colors and styles you like; you may be surprised. Don't worry if you feel resistance. That's natural. Once you get rolling, take some time to walk throughout your space and simply observe. Be sure to use all of your senses. Pay attention to how you feel.

- What do I love about my home? (Is it the light? The shape of the rooms?)
- Which characteristics made me choose this abode when I decided it was THE ONE? (Was it the view? The location? The price?)
- What about this space works for you? (The flow of the living space? The sense of security you have?)
- What is it about this space that never worked for me? (The lack of flow of the living space? The tiny kitchen?)

Don't share with anybody just yet. Sit with your answers for a bit and see what you notice. Let the emotions come up as they will. Don't judge them. Allow them to be as they are. I promise this information will be key in the transformation of your space and your life.

Now take your thinking deeper. Let your imagination run free. Consider these questions:

- Why do I want to create an oasis?
- Why is this important to me?
- What inspires me?
- Where am I now in my life?
- Does my stuff and my space represent that?
- Do I like what my current living environment says about me?

Again, just sit with your answers and don't judge them. You're not going to get in trouble. I'm certainly not going to yell at you. You're simply gathering information in order to know where you're at. These answers offer direction.

Once you step past your fear about what you might learn about yourself and your home, you've stepped into the possibility of having an exciting revelation about who you are and what you want around you. Every outcome is based on our expectations, plus our interpretation of the result. Some people get angry with themselves when they assess all that they have purchased and no longer enjoy. Or they are baffled by the items they once adored but now have no use for. Or they revert to useless shameful thoughts about how much they have. Together this all comes down to the belief that something is wrong with you.

Go take a look at some old photos of yourself from the 1980s. If you wore glasses then, your fashion statement frames would say something very different about you now and your prescription would certainly no longer benefit your vision. Sure, they probably cost you a bit of money then, but the only thing they are worth now is a chuckle for Throwback Thursday on your social media feed. Even with the cycles of fashion possibly bringing back that look, your taste and sense of style have changed along with the shape of your face. We accept this continual change without even being aware that we're making a choice. We recognize that our needs have shifted because we have shifted. In this instance, there is no judgment about it; it's part of living.

What if we looked at releasing these items that no longer serve us as a benchmark of growth? What if we could bring this same sense of peaceful acceptance to all the things that we only needed or enjoyed for a particular or temporary point in our lives but now only function as clutter? Why do we make ourselves wrong for growing? Why do we judge ourselves harshly for having different needs because of that growth?

I know, without a doubt, I'm not who I was ten years ago and most likely not even who I was five years ago. I look at this and get excited about who I will be in twenty years rather than focusing on the fact that I'll be seventy. I accept that what surrounds me now most likely won't in the future because my physical, technological and aesthetic needs will keep evolving and require different solutions.

These strategic questions create focus so you can begin to understand why you have clutter in your life and how it has taken over your home. Answering these questions gives you permission to accept change without judgment. This is where a shift occurs. I see it time and again with my clients, or even during casual conversations with people who ask about my work. The light finally goes on. The realization is transformative. You'll shift from clinging to items to letting them go in an instant.

THIS IS NOT PUNISHMENT

The clarity gained from this big shift in awareness frees us from suffering. There are a lot of feelings about what letting go of our stuff means. Most often those feelings are ones of struggle and suffering. I'm not sentencing you to a lifetime of restriction and self-denial or to live in an unalterable torture chamber with exactly one hundred objects (unless that's what you want, but I'm not teaching that here.) Instead, I'm equipping you to take back your own power which you have unconsciously given to your stuff. Rather than being filled with dread and shame, and being punished by cleaning up our clutter, we're waking up and becoming inspired to live with what we need for who we are now. Once we clearly see the things that aren't aligned with who we are now and where we are going, it's easier to let them go.

Incredibly, most people have no idea what they own. I see this when I sort through my clients' belongings with them. We often discover multiples of the same item that were repurchased because they couldn't remember where they put the first one. Repeatedly I hear: "Oh, that's where it was!" "I thought I lost this!" or "I've been looking for that!". This surprise is further proof of just how overwhelmed people are. The great news is no one needs to be that afflicted. It's possible to regain control of your space and your stuff by simply doing some self-study and determining whether the items you own are improving the quality of your life or holding you back.

As we work together, you'll discover what works for you so you don't waste time, energy and money having things or living in spaces that don't *feel* like you.

VISUALIZE

Before working with someone in their home, I send them a questionnaire. In it, I ask about their favorite colors, their favorite place in the world, their design style, and their hopes and dreams for their space. They might seem like simple questions, but they're essential. These questions help us to start creating a vision of what's possible. We focus on this because it lifts them out of where they are and places them on the path that's right for them. Once we have an idea of the destination, we begin to figure out how to get there.

Creating this vision can invite some fear. How can you be sure it's the right one? How can you be sure it's not going to be too complicated or overwhelming? What if I change my mind along the way? Good news! There is no wrong answer and the vision is usually quite easy to come up with. Here's an example of a powerful vision: "I want a functional kitchen because I'm tired of perpetually moving things around just to chop vegetables for dinner." This will mean ten different things to ten different people. One person might simply need to reorganize their cabinets so they can keep their counters clear. Another person might need a full kitchen renovation because they have no actual counter space. A vision is flexible and filled with many potential directions. It's also as individual as a fingerprint. Deep down you can trust that you have the answers. You know what you need and enjoy. As you go through the entire process, more and more details and options are revealed allowing your vision to grow organically along the way.

By shifting your immediate focus away from the clutter and disarray, and staying connected to your vision, you're discovering what's possible for you and your space. When the clutter starts to distract you as you begin this work and you get lost along the way, take a deep breath and return to your vision. It's the north star by which you can always navigate.

HOW DOES THIS MAKE ME FEEL?

Armed with your vision, you're ready to look at what surrounds you and how it makes you feel. Later on in the book, I will go into greater depth about the energy of objects, but for now, I want you to start to consider that you have a feeling about each and every item in your life. You may absolutely love it, feel completely neutral about it, or detest it. By questioning our feelings about the items around us, we start to realize how we allow our past emotions about an item to be the current experience of it.

Let's say you need more space in your closet, but there are several old outfits stashed in the back that you haven't worn in years, including the dress you wore the day you met your significant other, ten years ago. Many people are afraid to let go of that dress because they feel they are discarding the wonderful memory of that event along with the dress. But there's a difference between loving a dress for the memory it evokes and loving it because it's still an important staple of your wardrobe. Considering it's in the back of your closet and it's probably not seen the light of day in years, take a photo of it. Set an alarm in your calendar to look at the photo of the dress a month later and you will experience how the memories attached to the dress are also attached to the photo, which takes up way less space. This experiment usually inspires people to let go of the item and let it have another life outside of their closet.

A different example of confusing past emotions with present experience is furniture in your home you feel obligated to hold onto because of where it came from. Like the table from your dear departed grandmother you have in your hallway which you always bump into, and which no one else in your family has room for, becomes a burden instead of a positive connection to your personal history. This may sound obvious, but remember, your grandmother isn't that table. Needing a functional piece that fits your home and doesn't regularly bruise your shin doesn't mean you don't love and respect your grandmother's memory.

As you grow in awareness of the gap between past emotions and present experience, you'll grow more comfortable asking the question: How does this object make me feel now? You will be able to give yourself permission to become curious and make better choices about who you are at this moment in time and who you want to be in the future. Even so, strong negative emotions may still arise. You'll get scared and want to stop, and you forget all about your vision and growing awareness.

Then what?

WORKING THROUGH FEAR

One of the greatest rewards in my work is helping people see what's on the other side of their fear. Once we get past the fear and have released the tight grip it has on us, we see our imagined vision become our present physical reality. We've stepped into the future. Why was that so scary? It probably wasn't after all. What was scary was the anticipation and anxiety that you created around the idea of letting go and becoming a clutter-free person. That's usually the worst part. Most likely, this is where you've gotten stuck in the past. You knew you wanted something different, but you didn't know how to get there. Maybe you felt stupid, confused or just plain embarrassed about not knowing. But emboldened by your vision and increasing awareness, you're ready to work through your fear in a new way.

You can still expect fear to arise and that's normal. Here are three things to remember when your fear kicks in:

1. Fear is always a sign of growth. Resistance is always part of the territory.
2. You are only two chapters into this book. Right now, I'm just getting you primed so you can take meaningful action.
3. Most of the time, fear is your lizard brain creating reasons to hang on to something because letting go equals change. You are off to somewhere new and the amygdala wants to keep you protected. You won't be running into any saber-toothed tigers during this process, so thank your fears for trying to protect you and keep going.

When you start to feel afraid, connect with your awareness and stay curious. You can release the stronghold fear has over you and move forward in a direction that feels empowered.

CREATE AWARENESS TO CREATE CHANGE

When we bring our consciousness to specific areas of our life, change occurs. Why? Typically, we're on autopilot or simply reacting to the demands and pressures of our daily life and getting overwhelmed in our daily clutter. As awareness takes hold in your life things will get easier. You *know* which choices to make, maybe not all the time, but most of the time. You know what you desire. You know how you want to feel. You understand what lights you up. You see the bigger picture. And, on those days, when you lose sight of it, you know it's there.

Awareness is the first step to creating change.

Once you become aware, there's no going back.

3

WALKING THE TALK

HOW DOES THIS PLAY OUT IN MY LIFE?

Now that you're looking through the lens of awareness, you'll be happily surprised about how it grows and where it shows up in your life. In certain ways, your vision is expanding beyond the small picture of your own clutter and its impact on you, to the bigger picture of its impact on the world, and the health of the planet.

I know this is true for me.

Over the years, I have been able to observe how my growing awareness has affected my own choices and behavior for the better even though it has been uncomfortable at times. Here's a great example: Even though I have been a city-dweller for more than half of my life, I feel truly at home when I am near the ocean. I'd always dreamed of being a beach kid and repeatedly felt resentful that I couldn't live there year-round. In fact, I can only remember a few vacations in my entire life that didn't have the ocean as a destination. I love the salty sea air, the changing tides and playing in the water while my body moves with the waves. The vastness of the horizon reminds me of the endless possibilities in life. I must be truly present in the water. All my senses are activated and heightened especially when that unidentified "creature" touches my foot and I fly out of the water laughing and screaming my way to the safety of the beach.

I've always admired how clean the east coast beaches we visit are, as they get groomed each morning by caretakers gathering trash. I never gave much thought to where that trash was going while I enjoyed a pristine view for my pretty photos.

And then one day, rather dramatically, my awareness changed.

In 2016, I traveled to Eleuthera, an island in the Bahamas. During this vacation, we spent every single day snorkeling in and around a crystal-clear coral reef sixty steps down the cliff from the front door of our Airbnb. I've never experienced beauty like that before. Floating in magical and hypnotic turquoise waters, swimming through schools of fish that seemed too colorful to be real, I left my concrete-filled existence in Brooklyn behind. I felt like a child living inside an aquarium of exotic tropical fish.

One day, my husband and I hiked to the Atlantic Ocean side of the island and saw the spectacular beauty of Surfer's Beach. From a distance, it looked perfect. We couldn't wait to get closer. I wanted to capture this breathtaking beauty with my camera. As we raced down the dune to get a closer look, we realized something was wrong. Our steps slowed as reality hit. Hard. Washed up and piled on the shore were literally tons of plastic. The mounds of garbage went on for miles. I put my camera back in my bag. I didn't want to capture the horror. This was our perfect vacation and I wanted it to stay this way. Shaken by what we saw, and unable to truly take it in, we headed back to the cocoon of our pretty lagoon where we tried to bury our heads in the sand.

The image of that beach covered in plastic trash was burned in my brain. I couldn't unsee it. Later, I learned that these islands act as a filter and catch most of this decades-old garbage that had come from the United States. I wondered how much of this plastic was mine. Was that my 40-year-old headless Barbie doll sticking out of that endless heap of broken toys and junk on the shore?

This profoundly shifted my awareness of the relationship I had with my belongings. I'd never considered the responsibility, or lack thereof, that comes with the ownership of things in quite this way before. Whether it's my home, your own home, or our global home, we are each responsible for what fills it.

This is easy to forget.

I'm not sharing this to increase your anxiety or make you feel even more overwhelmed. Given how many responsibilities we face in any day - just trying to keep up with the notifications on our phones is a struggle! - most people are hardly able to keep up as it is. But by growing in your awareness of the care and disposal that the objects around you require, you'll start to ponder what you bring into your home, where it will live while you need it and where it will go when you are done with it.

For instance, take that slow cooker you thought you would use every day because it promised to change your life since it would encourage you to eat healthier, and also save you time and money because you would cook more often. You realize you only use it once a month, so it takes up valuable space as it's pushed into the back of the cabinet. Once the cabinet is bursting, that slow cooker gets moved down to the basement since you never really use it at all. Once some new shiny object captures your attention instead, you forget about it altogether. Then you remember it when you have to push past it, amidst all of the piles of other dust-covered forgotten promises of a better life, as you move more things to the basement to make room for that Instapot which promises the same thing only better and faster. And as you try to rearrange space for it, you stumble upon your mother's crockpot ... and then what? You can't just throw them all out.

Here you are, caught in the trap of your responsibilities.

Stay with me here; this isn't as dire as it sounds. With awareness of the responsibilities that our objects place on us, we can recognize the pattern of how they keep us stuck. My only goal is to give you permission to not only let go of items that are confining you but to put an end to this vicious cycle once and for all. Through your deepening awareness, you can choose which responsibilities you want to take on.

You can start to choose freedom instead of feeling trapped.

The choice between creating freedom or enabling a burden shows up in two areas which are often overlooked: shopping and convenience.

SHOPPING

Let's face it: Our hyperconnected world has us all stressed out and overloaded. Seeking some relief, even for a moment, we each have our individual ways of soothing ourselves. I know when I'm stressed or frustrated, peanut butter cups call my name loudly and repeatedly until I see the empty wrappers on my desk, and I can't even remember how they got there. This may be a step up from the days when I would shop for new shades of lipstick to add to my already overflowing makeup drawer. These purchases distracted me for a moment, but I was never satisfied for long. The next best plumping gloss would be unveiled the following week.

What I have found in my work is that most people who have a clutter problem turn to shopping to soothe themselves. Perhaps they feel unsatisfied in their home, their love life or in their jobs. Ultimately, buying something new is the pastime that is always available now more than ever before. It's the easiest way to avoid or ignore feelings that make us uncomfortable. Your office crush admires the photo of you and your boyfriend on your desk and, rather than eat lunch, you go to H & M and buy ten sweaters because they're buy-one-get-one-free which provides a safer thrill. Or your child's guidance counselor sends an email asking to meet and, the next thing you know, there's a pile of Amazon boxes outside your door.

For most of us, the magical part of buying something new happens just before the moment we approach the checkout or click the Place Order button. Excitement builds as we make the decision to make our purchase, anticipating just how much better and easier life and we will be after we own this object. Relief is on its way.

Here's the exact moment where we can also choose between creating freedom or enabling a burden. We have an opportunity to check-in before we check-out. By tuning into our awareness, and looking beyond this initial burst of excitement, we can stop, and pause, and think ahead. Maybe we ask these simple questions:

- Where will this go in my home?
- Do I really need this? (Really?)
- How much of my life will truly change with this purchase? (Will this make the meeting with the guidance counselor go away?)
- Is this bringing me closer to, or away from, my vision? (Remember that?)

By hitting pause and asking an objective question, you will snap you back into the present. By checking in with yourself, you will see if you're needlessly adding to your already overwhelmed life. I use these questions when I'm shopping and notice how often I really don't need what's in my cart. Most of the time, I discover I'm just looking for a distraction.

This isn't about making do with what we have or depriving ourselves, either. Sometimes you do need a new cute sundress and that's okay. By observing your behavior, you can better understand your habits and make informed decisions based on your vision. This process alone can be life changing. As your awareness grows, and your taste, expectations, and values become clear, you can't help but analyze your purchases in a different way.

One place this will begin to show up is around convenience.

CONVENIENCE

From the time I was a child in the early '70s until now, we've lived through a sea change in the way we shop. Never have so many brands, styles, and options been available to us in so many different ways. Just consider walking down the toothpaste aisle in the supermarket. How many kinds of toothpaste can there actually be? Can they all be that different? The choice can feel almost paralyzing. And that's just for toothpaste!

Many of us have transitioned to shopping online. The smartphone in your pocket is also your enormous personal shopping mall open for business 24/7. In so many ways this is wonderful. During super busy weeks, I'm happy to spend fifteen minutes placing my grocery order from the comfort of my home instead of spending three hours to go to the store, shop and come back. I love having the UPS driver deliver the bulky and heavy items I would've had to carry home on the subway. Convenience simplifies the choices we have now. All we have to do is type what we are looking for in the search box and hit enter to get what we need.

All this ease comes at a cost, however.

The cardboard boxes, plastic-wrapped everything, the delivery trucks on the road all have an impact on the environment. The effects of convenience on our society and the earth are drastic. Because this online lifestyle is still so new, as consumers, we can't fully comprehend all the consequences. But, as we take out our trash, we all understand that we're throwing away packing materials in larger quantities than we ever have before. This awareness is a good start, even though it's all so confusing and hard to look at. Our choices aren't clear.

I'm always looking for the "right" way to do things, and, in terms of caring for myself and nature, I always feel like I'm doing it wrong.

When I congratulate myself on planning my shopping ahead of time so I only get what I need, and avoid impulse purchases, I open the box that's delivered to my doorstep and it's filled with plastic packing materials and I wonder if it will ultimately wash up on that beach in Eleuthera. I believe in my heart there must be a better solution to this trade-off. Even if it hasn't been thought of yet, that doesn't mean it won't be.

I'm not sure what the answer is, but I know talking about it is better than not. As I've been sharing my questions with others, so many new alternatives are coming into my awareness. People send me articles about the new biodegradable straw or Instagram adds a new eco-friendly alternative onto my feed. As hard as it is to look at these issues, it's the next best step in making room for new solutions to appear. By inviting you to ask these questions of yourself, together we can magnify and multiply the opportunities and solutions that will show up for all of us and future generations.

I'm not saying this process will be fool-proof and it isn't about being perfect. As we all have more moments of awareness and begin to assess how our purchases, including the packaging they come in, are cluttering up our brains, personal space, and the planet, we are liberated from being continually overwhelmed. We are free to make the very easy shifts that create genuine change in our lives which can restore health and balance in our homes and on the planet.

4

IDENTIFYING BELIEFS & HABITS

As we cultivate the awareness of being able to make different choices and grow comfortable with the possibility that we can change our reality, we will start to look at our beliefs and habits in a new light as well. Our beliefs and habits aren't always easy to identify because our subconscious mind rules them. Beliefs and habits are like the operating system in our computers which are constantly running in the background. We don't notice or recognize them, and never think to question them.

They're just there.

Which is why I may ask a client "Why did you decide to set up the kitchen this way?" The usual response is, "I never thought about it. This is just the way it's supposed to be. It's the way it's always been. It's the way my family did it. It's what I'm supposed to do." These kinds of beliefs, and the habits that they create, are what most of us have blindly accepted as the truth about our homes. Without realizing it, we also accept the limitations in our homes placed on us by these beliefs and habits. It's what we become used to, even if they don't allow us to function effectively in our spaces.

Your operating system is overdue for an update, don't you think? So, let's dig a little deeper into what beliefs and habits are. Then you can see how they govern how you live in your home.

WHAT ARE BELIEFS?

A belief is an idea that we have repeated in our minds, usually from an early age, which has never been questioned. A person or an experience taught it to us to keep us safe or make us feel better. I happen to believe I am lucky. I have believed this for as long as I can remember. Seeking the source of this belief, I recalled a memory of when I was three years old on a ferry ride. To pass the time, my father had bought a bunch of scratch-off lottery tickets. Comfortably perched in my father's arms, he watched with delight as I scratched away. Winner! With every ticket he gave me, I'd win again. "Sweetie", he said each time, "you are lucky!" And I've lived life expecting luck ever since.

My mom and grandmother believed I was a sloppy kid and always told me so. While I loved being called lucky, being called a slob didn't feel good. One day when I was about nine or ten years old, I decided to prove them wrong. My mom asked me to clean up my room and I went *all out*. On that particular day, I got in there and I went through EVERYTHING. We're talking stuffed animals, random game pieces, toys I'd lost interest in, clothing. I filled up an entire garbage bag with all I didn't need and didn't want and put it in the hallway outside of my room. This bag was undeniable evidence that I wasn't a sloppy kid after all. It was proof that if I put my mind to it, I could create a beautiful space.

I distinctly remember the pride I felt in this great accomplishment. I knew in my heart that by letting go of these things, I was also releasing the label of being a slob. I discovered that I could create who I wanted to be. I had the power over my stuff instead of my stuff having power over me. As I sat in my room and looked around at the clear space that I had created, I could finally breathe. It was bliss! I excitedly called for my mom to come and see my perfectly cleaned up room. I couldn't wait to surprise her with my metamorphosis into a tidy person!

But the bag in the hallway stopped her in her tracks.

She opened it up and saw the stuff that I no longer needed, going through the items one by one as she scolded me for throwing away "perfectly good things." The entire bag was ultimately *given* to my brother. The poor kid, he didn't want any of it either. Without even realizing it, a new belief was created for me, the same one so many of us have in our lives that play out as "It's wasteful to get rid of things." The bag in the hallway that I knew was proof of my liberation transformed into evidence that I was ungrateful for all that I had.

In looking at this story I have compassion for my mother as she was only one generation away from family members who lived through the Great Depression, wartime and poverty. They didn't throw things away. The very idea of doing so was preposterous. What would possess you to throw things away? Most of us are programmed with these beliefs without even realizing it. The Great Depression ended in 1941. That's not so long ago. And most of us still carry the beliefs from that era in our DNA which hasn't caught up with the abundance epidemic in which we currently live. No wonder we have so much trouble with letting go.

With the awareness we are developing we can get a clear sense of beliefs that were given to us in childhood versus the beliefs formed by our lived experience as adults. Now we can look back at our beliefs and the behaviors and actions by which they are expressed and start to question them. We can choose the beliefs that are aligned with who we are now or who we want to be.

Here are some examples of beliefs that show up in connection with our belongings:

1. **I believe in my guilt.**
    If I get rid of this ugly vase from my aunt, which I never use and which is now taking up space in the back of a kitchen cabinet, not only will I hurt her feelings, I will forget about her. I'm throwing away our relationship. I deserve to feel guilty because this proves I'm ungrateful. Ask yourself: Is this actually true? Do you need the physical object that you never use to keep a memory of a loved one? An object that you are ambivalent about keeps you ambivalent about the person. Is that how you really want to be reminded of them? Aunt Jane = ugly vase. Who is determining and judging whether our behavior is good or bad? We need to have the expectation that our possessions keep us buoyant, not burdened.

2. **I believe this item only serves one purpose.**
    I have a dresser in my bedroom. I put my clothes in it. Because that's where a dresser belongs and what it's for. But, since the drawers are too shallow, the clothes never fit properly so I wrestle them open and they never shut properly. Not only that, the dresser is too big for the room. It would fit better in my hallway and provide the perfect space to become the home base solution that holds everything I need when I leave for the day. But I can't put it there because a dresser belongs in the bedroom filled with clothes. Is this really true? Wouldn't it be better to move the dresser into the hallway and restructure the bedroom closet with deeper drawers? By adding drawers in the closet, you'll create more space in the bedroom. With the dresser near the front door, you have everything you need to go to work in the morning housed in one convenient place.

3. **I believe I should keep this forever.**
    I bought a treadmill after my physical two years ago as I was committing to finally get in shape. Now that I've joined a

walking club in my neighborhood, I'm not inspired to use it. However, because I spent good money on it and there's an infinitesimal chance that I might use it again, I can't get rid of it. (Also, it's become the perfect place to throw my clothes that I don't feel like putting away.) Is this true? Does this suit my life now? Do I need it now? When was the last time I used this? Is this really the best place to hang my clothes? Couldn't I make better use of the space it's taking up? These questions not only apply for the objects you already have but can also offer a new perspective while you're shopping. By no longer looking at our stuff as a life-sentence, it allows us to assess the reality of how long we will use the item and if it's worth the expense.

By continuing to question your beliefs, you will better understand their validity. Some powerful questions to start with are:

- Do I really believe this?
- Was I influenced at an early age by a person in my life who judged me?
- Was I taught that there's only one way to do something?
- Where does this belief limit my life?

As you grow more comfortable asking these questions, you'll have the most important realization that most of your beliefs are coming from a place of lack.

Behind the belief of "I might need it someday" is a deeper belief of not having enough. Our lizard brain is hard at work on this one. It's the fear that we won't have access or the funds to get what we need in the future. And this fear can be justified with the belief that "It will increase in value." Armed with these beliefs, we give ourselves permission to hold on, letting ourselves off the hook from the poor choices we've made while cementing us firmly in the past. These beliefs don't change the fact that our items are still taking up space. These beliefs also don't change the fact that, unless you are educated in a particular niche, have done your research, kept the items in pristine condition, and know there is a buyer looking for this particular "collector's item," nine times out of ten, a quick search on eBay reveals that there are many other people out there holding on to the same item. Like you, they also believed it would increase in value only to discover the bids on it never move past two bucks.

Having tested your beliefs through investigative efforts you can determine if they will truly support the vision of how you want to live now. The clear answers you find will highlight where your beliefs need to be modified. This is a process of lining up your beliefs with how you want to live. If you truly want to be organized, the first step is to believe that it is possible. When your priority becomes living in order your beliefs will shift. Remember, too: this is a gradual process, one to keep trying on to see how it fits, and which is continually adjusted as you and your life evolve. Beliefs are the starting point to get the place that feels better and is aligned with where you are now.

Create the belief, then the habit will follow.

WHAT IS A HABIT?

Habits are behaviors formed by both our beliefs and our environment. Typically, they too are subconscious and involuntary. Some habits, like where we take off our shoes, the place we drop our keys, or the way we move around our home are a default response; they're what we do because it's what we've always done. Other habits are learned such as looking both ways before crossing the street or making the bed in the morning. Our homes are the incubator of our habits, good and bad, and reflect what is or isn't working in them.

I always have my clients walk me through exactly what happens when they come home from work:

- what do they have in their hands?
- where do they put them?
- what do they do next?

These are very easy answers for my clients to share as they repeat these steps daily seemingly without thinking. The good news is that the habit reveals where the solution is needed. It's easier to create a solution around the habit than to change the habit. As an example, one of my clients had a never-ending pile of mail, receipts, and bags on his kitchen table as well as an assortment of shoes underneath it. He wanted to come home and let go of the stress of his workday. Instead, he was greeted by piles of more things that needed to be taken care of. The entry to his home was through the kitchen. Every day, he rushed through it, dropping whatever was in his hands, and kicking off his shoes, as he made his way to his bedroom at the back of his apartment so he could get out of his suit as quickly as possible. He never came back to deal with what he left on the table and by the end of the workweek, he was too tired to address the mess.

We easily solved his frustration by adding shelves above the table. We outfitted them with containers for the mail, receipts and a hook for his keys. A new shoe rack by the door helped my client save time in the morning because he could easily select the pair he needed. Now that we cleared a path and assigned a place for all his important things, he could relax in his home and fully enjoy it. Simply by observing his individual habits, we created customized solutions. These solutions were easy to implement and were successful because he didn't have to change his habits. This offered the relief he'd been seeking rather than more struggle and failure.

While preserving the household's current habits is the priority when first solving a clutter or space issue, sometimes they will have to be modified because of spatial or physical limitations. For example, I had another client who works from home. Her desk was in her bedroom and it partially blocked the closet door which couldn't be opened fully making it a challenge to put away her clothes. Rather than fight the closet door every night, she would throw her clothes on the desk chair. When she needed to sit at her desk in the morning, the pile would then go to her bed only to then become a pile in the corner on the floor when it was time to go to sleep.

Because she could never find anything to wear, she often shopped for more clothing, eventually creating a bigger pile and a bigger problem.

Like most of us, she inadvertently created a chain of habits that were making life more difficult. Needing a temporary solution - *I'm in a rush, I'll just put my clothes on this chair for now* - she didn't consider that this would become her standard operating procedure, snowballing into a serious clutter issue. By taking the time to rearrange her bedroom furniture, we were able to give her easy access to her closet, but clearly it was still up to her to create a new habit for the solution to work. While not easy at first, her frustration motivated her to adopt the new habits needed to live and work more comfortably in her home.

Please remember this is not an overnight change. These are all gradual steps and processes which grow along with us. Yes, there will be days when you throw the clothes on the chair and a pile starts to form. Strengthened by these new beliefs and habits, you'll recognize a problem in the making before it gets out of hand and choose to take five minutes to get your home back in order.

We have to be kind to ourselves along the way especially when lapses occur. As our beliefs shifts and the habits follow, it will all become second nature.

5

SENSING ENERGY

W hat do gravity, electricity, and the internet have in common? We don't have to see or understand them for them to have a daily effect on us. Usually, we don't even think about or notice them until we fall down, or the lights go out, or the cable fails, and we can't stream *The Morning Show*. They're invisible and complicated. We can't function in the world today without them. They've become our silent partners.

Energy is another silent partner that is rarely considered. Whether we realize it or not, energy is constant and affecting us all of the time. This is particularly true in our homes because every object in it holds energy. The surge of good feeling you experience as you look at the collage of photos of your children is energy. The sleepy sensation of lethargy you experience when you look at the bulging boxes of unsorted files spilling onto the floor is also energy. Because that pile feels stagnant, you feel stagnant. Because that pile feels heavy and dense, you feel heavy and dense. And because that closet feels jammed, you feel jammed. At its simplest level, this is all I mean when I talk about clearing space: finding practical ways to release energy that is stuck which is, in turn, keeping you stuck.

Now that you have grown in awareness, created your vision, are shopping mindfully, and examined your beliefs and habits, you're probably starting to notice how you feel about what surrounds you

37

even if you haven't been able to label it. You are sensing energy. It's the step that illuminates the work we're about to do.

But, first, let's take a closer look.

THE HOW OF ENERGY

Try this experiment: After you finish your laundry, pair up and fold half of your socks and place them on one side of the drawer. On the other side, just dump in the remaining unmatched socks. As the week goes by, notice the following:

- Which side are you drawn to?
- Which do you return to?
- How do you feel when you engage with each side?
- Which gives you a sense of ease or pleasure?
- Which causes unnecessary stress?

Like many readers of this book, you most likely had positive feelings about the side of the drawer with the folded socks. (If you didn't notice anything, don't be concerned. Maybe socks aren't your issue. Try the same experiment with your earrings.) You enjoyed the ease and sensation of flow this added to your morning routine. The simple experiment shows the shift in energy we can create in minutes.

Imagine how this plays out on a larger scale in your home. For example, I had a client who always felt she couldn't move forward in her life. Often, she described herself as feeling trapped. I met with her in her home and immediately noticed that there was an abundance of boxes literally blocking her path in the entryway and living room. She's a busy professional who handled most of her shopping online. She couldn't keep up with opening the boxes, putting the items away, and getting the empty boxes to the recycling bin. As the number of boxes grew, literally taking up her space, and shrinking the room she had to live in, it was no wonder she felt she couldn't move forward.

To soothe herself, she turned to more shopping, not realizing how this coping mechanism was actually creating more stagnant energy, keeping her stuck where she was, overwhelmed and burdened. By having my assistants empty, break down and remove the boxes, the energy in the room suddenly shifted. Because she now felt less closed in and could see for herself how simple efforts could affect change, her energy came alive with a sense of possibilities. I could see the relief and freedom she was beginning to feel. As we continued working together over the next few weeks, she started to expand her life in ways she hadn't before. She was planning vacations and making dates with friends to see shows. She started shopping less. She mentioned how surprised she was by how much felt possible in her life now.

But I wasn't surprised.

Unblocking and stirring up all of the heavy, stagnant energy always brings new and fresh energy into your life. This may sound kind of *out there* for some of you, but let's look at it directly: we receive and feel the positive energy from the things we appreciate, enjoy wearing and use regularly; we receive and feel the negative energy from things that we no longer enjoy, use, or need. Think about how frustrated you feel every time you have to root through all of those clothes that no longer fit. Without even knowing it, we infuse our objects and homes with negative energy. Things like boxes, shopping bags, and junk mail belong in the recycle bin and not in the front hallway. When we begin to see how holding onto things that belong in the garbage only invites more garbage into our lives, we can create new beliefs and habits to help ourselves.

SPACE AND ENERGY

Once we accept that objects hold energy, we can explore how our space does too and how that energy affects us. We underestimate or rarely think about how important this energetic flow is. As we move through our spaces daily, pathways emerge, some of which work for us and some of which don't. I pay very close attention when moving through someone's space for the first time. My job is to analyze the space and see where my client is being held back. Even though my client appears comfortable moving through her space, I'll notice immediately she's navigating an obstacle course.

Like when she crouches to avoid the hanging plant each time, she passes through the living room. When I ask if it bothers her to duck each time, her response is "What do you mean, when did I duck?" Interestingly, she then remarked how tired she was. She wished she could just relax instead of always being on high alert. Here's where I point out to her that she won't be able to relax in her home while she has to navigate obstacles. If she spends her day having to avoid hitting her head, it's no wonder she feels under attack all the time. It makes sense that she's worn out.

The energy of her home is dictating it. It's not functional, so it's difficult for her to be functional.

Once we reoriented her space, she was surprised how much better she felt. It's no wonder. The energy can flow freely without obstructions. We've dismantled a chain reaction. Because the furniture was in the wrong place, the energy collected and grew stagnant which, in turn, attracted more stagnant energy in the form of clutter.

Sometimes all that's needed to invite fresh energy in are some quick changes. Something as easy as turning a table ninety degrees can produce an immediate and transformative effect. The ease of having a direct route to the bedroom may show up in having more restful night's sleep or just a sense of well-being. Think about where you would like more flow in your home, and what physical objects could be the culprits in preventing that from happening.

While these solutions are often straightforward, sometimes there are more complex energetic shifts in a room, usually following a change in our lives. Since we are constantly changing, there will always be certain times when our pattern of life is disrupted such as:

- Starting a new exercise routine or diet
- Marriage or moving in together
- Change of job or starting to work from home
- Getting a pet
- Having a baby
- Empty nest
- Someone dies

What all of these scenarios have in common is that your home now needs to evolve, inviting you to be in your home in a different way than you've ever been before. The choices you make must be based on where you are going, not where you were. These life changes are prime situations for clutter to either begin or grow. By not recognizing the consequences of change, and not understanding these choices we have to make, we become stuck between worlds and the energy grows stagnant.

This is where trouble can start.

Clearly these examples are stressful because anything out of the ordinary will trigger our old friend, the lizard brain (DRAMA!). Even happy life events carry their own risk because, although we want to invite these transitions into our lives, we still fear the unknown. We struggle trying to live old patterns which no longer fit our new situation and block the new energy that change brings.

Let's dig deeper into an example of transitioning to work from home. Once a home also becomes a workplace, the energy of the home transforms significantly. The space needs to include the energy of work and an area to contain it. Worlds are colliding. Imagine that your office persona is now moving into your house. You need your own space to feel comfortable and flourish while not interfering with the nurturing qualities of home, which are necessary to recharge after a long workday.

To support that shift, it's important to have a specific area from which to work, especially if there isn't a spare room available to create an office. By giving our work-self a space, which honors our tasks, it shows that we honor and respect our business and our clients. More importantly, it sets up a much-needed boundary between work-self and home-self which is more necessary than anyone realizes until it's too late.

I've learned this the hard way.

I've worked from home more often than not during my various careers. Back in the late nineties, I set up my office in my bedroom because that was the only place my small desk would fit in my seven hundred square-foot apartment. Even though I got regular sleep, I was always exhausted. I attributed that feeling to the stress of building my struggling business. When I moved to Brooklyn in late 2001 and was finally able to create a workspace in another area of my home, a funny thing happened.

Sleep came easily. I felt rested. I thought about work when I was at my desk, not in bed. It was then I realized the impact of not separating the energies of work and rest. Subconsciously, in my old apartment, I had always been aware of the presence of work even when I was supposed to be resting. I couldn't turn off my brain easily. Walking into my bedroom when I was ready for bed, I would instantly be reminded about what I could be doing or what I hadn't accomplished that day. I never had to worry about the monsters hiding under the bed, because the giant desktop computer sitting directly in my line of vision was scary enough. I wish I had thought to cover it when I finished my workday to remind myself when I went to bed that I was off the clock.

Another way of confusing the energy of your work-self and home-self may show up when using the dining room table as a desk. Perhaps that began as a temporary solution. But that was three years ago. As a result of this "temporary" solution, the family habits have shifted. Rather than connecting and sharing a meal together, your family formed new habits like eating individually at different times, or in front of the television or other screens. Let's say you all needed to sit at the table together for a holiday or birthday. Your partner had to move your piles of paper and files to make room. And now you can't find the business card of the potential new client you just met, who you promised to contact to discuss a time-sensitive project. The energy in this space has become a hotbed for misunderstandings because there are no clear boundaries between home and work. No one is sure if this is a space for the family to be together or space for private work.

This lack of clarity shows up in the energies of frustration and resentment; the room always feels tense. This is effortlessly fixed, however. By having a conversation about how and when everyone needs to use this space, manageable solutions and systems can be created to keep the flow of energy free and moving. The walls of our home seldom change, but our priorities, and the choices we need to make about what happens within those walls, do. With your growing awareness of what your shifting needs require, your space will better reflect them. The energy of your home will stay fresh and aligned.

Re-evaluating your space and how you utilize and live in it is expected to be an ongoing part of your life. By not doing so, you'll hold onto things that become lifeless and fill your home with dormant energy in the form of clutter. Remember: you are a continual work in progress. If you welcome that growth with curiosity and conversation, instead of frustration, new worlds open. By focusing on what you need, energy flows in the direction of your desires. It is the most remarkable way to transform your home and life.

6

DEFINING VALUE

How do you know what something is truly worth?

This is the hard question many people run up against in our work together. Typically, it also presents the biggest stumbling block on the path to realizing their vision. Because everyone has their own unique method of defining value based on their current emotions, bank account balance, along with their upbringing and beliefs, questions of worth invite the greatest amount of resistance.

I am fascinated by the broad and complicated interpretations of value that I work through with my clients. Over the years, I've observed three areas where people get stuck on their way to becoming clutter-free. It's likely that you may get stuck in one of these, too. In order to help keep up your momentum during your work, let's take a look at these areas so you are prepared to handle them once you begin. In this chapter, we will look at the complex and personal ways we assign value to what we own or would like to own. We will also examine the value we assign to time. Most importantly, we will look at how we do or do not value ourselves. Understanding how these three kinds of value interact are the key to your success in taking control of your stuff.

THE VALUE OF OBJECTS

It is hard to arrive at a universal agreement on the true value of anything as we all have a different interpretation of worth based on . . . well . . . our values. But my clients all agree that some of what's cluttering their home is worth *something*. They are quite clear about that. Someone will point to the "antique" rocking chair that's sole function is to hold the coats heaped upon it because it's blocking the closet. It must have value simply because they've had it a long time and has been passed down for generations (but was really purchased at the neighborhood yard sale, and now the seat is busted and needs several hundred dollars for a repair to make it functional).

"Smith, I *know* this chair has to be worth *something*! I can't get rid of it." Trust me, I have heard every variation of this example. Each time, it reminds me of how vulnerability and confusion are hiding under people's perception of value. This vulnerability and confusion show up as resistance expressed through bargaining. The usual suspects of bargaining are:

- **I know this is worth something.** Like the "antique" rocking chair mentioned above, there are plenty of objects in your home you could point to and make the same argument. Fed by a steady diet of *Antiques Roadshow* and *Storage Wars*, there are many ways we are led to believe holding on to something increases our chances of sitting on an undiscovered goldmine. But really, are your warped baseball cards and moldy books going to appreciate in value over time? Are you going to invest the money and time to get them in saleable condition, money and time which you may not recoup? Letting go of the item is ultimately the easiest way to save time, money and reclaim precious space.
- **I got a deal on it.** Everyone loves getting a bargain and the idea of saving money it represents. Black Friday and every other holiday sale are classic examples of exploiting that love, fanning the flames of our desire. We're more focused

on getting that special offer meant just for us than the item itself. The sense of pride we take in the deal stops us from wondering how many flatscreen TV's we actually need. For years, my husband and I have joked when either of us bought something only because it was on sale, "Look, honey, I saved money!" Don't you love telling someone who's commented on the fabulous sweater you're wearing that it only cost twenty bucks on sale? It's an ego boost and makes us feel special to have found the deal. And it makes us feel good to have "saved money." Only suckers pay retail, right?! It's those feelings that determine the value of these objects and what keeps us attached to them.

- **I spent good money on this.** Alternatively, once a purchase has been made of an item that we paid full price for, well . . . "I can't get rid of that, I spent good money on it!" Isn't that how you justify those designer leather pants you bought on the day you were dumped by your boyfriend to remind yourself how sexy you really are, even though that was six years ago, and you've never worn them since you became Senior Vice President in your company, and you've come to realize you're just not a leather pants kind of gal? Even knowing this, you find it hard to let go because you paid full price. Letting go may feel like you made a mistake and opens the door to beating yourself up for having made an impulse purchase in a moment of weakness. But you can let go of those feelings too.

- **I might need it someday.** The rowing machine under the bed from 1998. The instruction manual and bits of extra electrical parts from the ceiling fan that was installed ten years ago. The tangled charging cord for your first flip phone. Enough said.

- **I'd break my mother's heart if I gave this away.** I just lived this one out with a surprise ending. I have wine glasses that I thought were "passed down for generations." I hate them. I've only used them once or twice. They have hollow stems that are difficult to clean and always look dirty. My husband doesn't like them either. He's the wine drinker in the

47

family and those glasses are too dainty for his man-hands. I'd always wanted to get rid of them but didn't because I thought it would break my mother's heart. After hosting a recent dinner party, I was reminded of how much I detested those glasses. I realized that I was bargaining with myself and was caught in the trap of determining value. Trying to practice what I preach, I texted my mother a photo of them and said, "What's the deal with these wine glasses?" She replied immediately, "Those were Mema's (her mother), they have a hollow stem. I forgot about them. So cool!" I cursed silently, expecting her to say they were valuable or please don't get rid of them, BUT SHE FORGOT ALL ABOUT THEM. I could have quietly let them go years ago. Instead, I let the story of their imagined value become a burden and a source of resentment. (Happy ending . . . she said please don't throw them out, but you can donate them, which I did the very next day!)

People don't expect me to continue questioning them after they've told me their idea of an object's value. But I do because I know this item will remain a clutter magnet. This is where the bargaining gets more intense: they'll only agree to let go if they can sell it for what they believe it's worth. I'm happy to help them do that and guide them through a series of gentle questions in order to make that happen:

- Have you sold anything before?
- Who might buy this?
- Would you say it's in perfect condition?
- If not, what are the costs for any needed repairs?
- Where will you sell it?
- How will you transport or ship it once it's sold?
- Have you factored in the cost of shipping?
- Have you considered what happens if it gets lost or damaged en route?

At this point, their eyes widen as they realize that the idea of the value that they're holding onto has become quite complicated.

"But what about this lamp though?" they ask as they excavate it from a pile in the corner. The finish is chipped. The shade is damaged.

"*I know* it's valuable, it just needs a few repairs," they say.

While lamp repair is certainly a possibility, I only recommend repairing the items we know for certain can be sold, not the items we *think* we can sell. If selling that lamp is truly your goal, then a quick search on eBay will show what the lamp is worth right now. Voila! With the click of a button, you can see how many of them are currently for sale, what the going rate is, comparisons of the quality, make, model, year and see if there is actually a buyer for it. Seeing the thirty other lamps selling at twenty-five dollars or less is enough of a reality check for most people to move the item to the donation pile. But for the sincere believers, I give them a copy of the very long list of what's required to sell an item, created by my brother who has successfully sold many items over the years on eBay. It includes everything: market research, how to take the right photo, what to include in the description, monitoring the auction, how to collect the payment, packing, insurance, and shipping. (And that's just for the first item.) Phew! It's definitely not for novices. Sometimes taking the ten minutes to think through all this tedious work allows them to realize what truly is valuable: their time.

THE VALUE OF TIME

Underneath these ideas we've been exploring in the first chapters, is the big question of time and the sense of not having enough of it. This question is usually what inspires people to remake their relationship to their stuff; they're spending too much time managing their stuff or avoiding managing their stuff, rather than living their lives. They are tired of the stress of always being late to work because they had to wash the pot that's sitting in the sink full of dirty dishes in order to make breakfast, or couldn't find the matching sock they needed, or spent too much time searching for their keys they left in a different purse. Somewhere they sense that all of those wasted moments must add up in a lifetime. According to *US News and World Reports*, average Americans are known to spend one year of their lives searching for lost or misplaced items.

Hearing about my clients' struggles demonstrates their confusion about how they value their time since they don't feel as though they are in control of their lives and schedules. Confessions like "I'm always late for work" or "I can never find what I need in the morning" or "I've nothing to wear" or "I don't have time to cook meals or time to shop" tells me they are living by default, allowing outside elements to dictate their schedule. Rather than understanding the worth of their time they've allowed others and circumstances to determine it for them. The habit of moving the same pile of clothes every day becomes the unconscious measure of what their time is worth.

I teach them to understand that they, and not their stuff or situation, determine the value of their time. They choose how they want to spend it. Once they fully appreciate how valuable their time is, they don't want to waste it moving the same pile of clothes every day. I like to show my clients how something as simple as making a cup of coffee is an opportunity to discover the value of time. I ask them to walk me through their process of making coffee every morning. It's amazing how many circles they'll walk around their kitchen to perform this seemingly simple task. The mugs are in a cabinet nowhere near the coffeemaker. The spoons are three more steps away. The refrigerator holding the cream is on the far side of the kitchen. That's a lot of steps! Good for the Fitbit, bad for valuing your time.

Which leads to the burning question, how much do you value your time?

The interesting thing about time is that it can be created. In order to accomplish any goal, you have to claim the time you need to achieve it. In the fall of 2017, I had an overwhelming desire to share my knowledge beyond my circle of clients. I had a million good reasons for why I didn't have time to write a book. I was juggling several clients and besides my responsibilities to them, there were all of my other responsibilities including my networking, administrative duties, household duties, family and volunteer time. I was feeling quite busy. It didn't seem possible at all. But my need to get this information out of my head and into people's hands wouldn't leave me alone. I had seen so many examples of distress that had simple solutions if only people had the information available to them. I wanted to help but there were only twenty-four hours in a day, and I felt maxed out already. I had to make a choice about how I was valuing my time. I started waking up at six in the morning and wrote for one or two hours consistently. In two weeks, I had over seventeen thousand words which gave me the confidence and momentum to continue. What did I discover? Time spent mindlessly scrolling on the internet or watching another Netflix series until one in the morning couldn't compare with the value of time spent creating something and expressing myself. It was an easy choice once I learned what I truly valued.

When you invest your time gaining awareness of what your time is actually worth, it will be a game-changer. Is your time more valuable than trying to find your car keys every day? Or digging through your winter clothes to find a tank top on a hot summer day? Of course it is! And it feels good, too. I remember working with a client who had a large bag of clothing that needed to be repaired. Because she was handy with a needle and thread, she kept insisting she'd do the mending herself. Which she never did. Every time she looked at the bag she felt like she was being lazy for not taking care of it but also felt like she didn't have time to do it. Even though these two thoughts don't add up, when combined, they are a trap. They create the perfect opportunity to waste time beating yourself up. Once we discussed how long it would actually take her to mend all of these clothes, not to mention the time lost stressing about it, the choice to drop them off to be repaired the next time she dropped off her dry cleaning was a no-brainer. After she made this simple choice, she was surprised by the relief she felt. She realized just how stuck she had been wasting her time feeling bad. She had a new appreciation for the value of her time and the pleasure of letting a professional help her.

She gained awareness about how she actually was spending her time versus how she wanted to spend it. This was a turning point to which she'd never return. I made the same discovery when I was first living on my own. I never ever wanted to do the dishes. Ever. It was hard to enjoy the meal I had just prepared with the chore of doing the dishes looming over me. Even if I ate in the living room in front of the television, there was no escape from those dishes. I would spend at least an hour and a half thinking about how much I didn't want to do them.

One day I couldn't take the constant complaining in my head about the damn dishes anymore. I wasn't willing to live like this for the rest of my life; it's not like I was going to stop cooking or eating. It occurred to me that I spent an enormous amount of time feeling bad about not doing the dishes when I didn't even know how long it took to wash them. So, I did an experiment.

I looked at the clock. Did the dishes. Done. Time? SIX MINUTES.

What?!!

I've been wasting hours of my life in anticipation of something that takes minutes to do. That changed me forever. I couldn't go back after learning that lesson. Now I really knew I had to choose how I spent my time. Time spent in my head wrestling with my thoughts and beliefs was time spent not living. It was time wasted on meaningless anxiety keeping me stuck and preventing me from enjoying even simple things like the delicious home-cooked meal I made.

The more we observe how we spend our time, the more educated decisions we will make about how we want to use it. Knowing this, here's where you're going to have to make the decision about investing your time in order to get organized. It's going to feel like not wanting to do the dishes. Your inner brat will fully show up, stamp her feet, and say, "I don't wanna do it!" Don't be fooled. Just realize that's not your inner brat at all. It's only your lizard brain in a cheap Halloween costume trying to scare you so things stay things just as they are.

After the tantrum passes, ask exactly how much more of your precious time you're willing to waste on feeling bad about yourself. The answer will be a clue about how you value yourself.

THE VALUE OF OURSELVES

How is choosing to ignore your clutter a reflection of how you value yourself?

If you're like most of my clients, you may never have thought about this connection before. And it still may feel uncomfortable to examine how your thoughts and beliefs are so deeply intertwined with inanimate objects. But since you've gotten this far, I can tell you're starting to recognize how the stuff that blocks your energy is preventing you from feeling better. You're connecting these dots more easily. You've grown curious about how your subconscious really feels about your stuff.

I'm excited that you're ready to make how you feel in your space a priority.

Have you ever thought about how relaxed you feel in a nice hotel? You might think it's because of the luxurious linens, fresh towels, and fancy good smelling bath products (which I'm certain you brought home with you to add to your hotel toiletry collection). Or maybe you believe that simply because you are on vacation, you're finally able to unwind and recharge. You know deep down you're in a place where you can rest. And while those carefully chosen details contribute to that sense of peace, it's a result of the environment and how it was designed to function. Moreover, you're away from all of the extraneous physical stuff that is wearing you down. Think about it for a moment. You only have what you need. You know where everything is. The bed is made. Because everything has a place, you don't have to make any decisions. You're not thinking about your stuff; you're only thinking about your day. You can give your brain a rest and just *be*.

Can you imagine your home feeling that way? Can you imagine living in a space that feels peaceful and restorative? Don't you even feel better just thinking about that possibility? If the sense that it's possible to live that way excites you, congratulations, you're choosing to value yourself. You're recognizing your own worth. You're recognizing that you deserve a home that is nourishing. Choosing to live this way is choosing the ultimate self-care.

Moms, I'm talking directly to you here.

How can you expect to take care of everyone else if you aren't making your well-being in your home environment a priority? I know this may sound like more work for you to do, but I promise that, once you decide to value how you feel in your home, you'll be able to take care of your family when you don't feel depleted and resentful everyday.

The resistance you may feel about taking on this work is real. I see it all the time. You're facing what seems like a million decisions you don't know how to make. You don't know where to begin. You're afraid you'll be doing it wrong. And you doubt that you have the skills and time to even start. I mean there were all those other past efforts that lead nowhere.

I'm going to let you in on another secret.

The physical work you are avoiding is a sign of the emotions you are afraid of feeling. The guilt and shame people feel about the stuff they have spent money on and no longer use runs deep. It's scary,

54

in the same way taking a stand for your value is scary. Most of us would rather shove everything back in the closet than to truly face it. Yes, that fear may seem real, but it can't hurt you. Really. It's only your tricky amygdala showing up in another clever disguise trying to protect you. This is a false sense of security.

The solution to all of this is understanding that you are allowed to feel good. You are allowed to make yourself feel better. Misunderstanding the value of your objects, time, and yourself is a subtle form of self-abuse. This misunderstanding has a profound negative effect on you without you even realizing it.

If you don't feel good in your space, look through the lens of worthiness. You deserve something as simple as a good night's sleep in your own home which you aren't going to get in a home full of chaos. You can start over with a space that truly inspires and delights you.

Everyone is worthy of living this way.

It's simple magic. You must believe you deserve it. Once you do, then you are ready to begin.

7

LET GO

―――――

LETTING GO - A STORY

After graduating from college, I was finally moving from my childhood home in the Hudson Valley to live with some friends on Long Island. I was ready, or so I thought, to be a real adult in the big world. I fantasized about getting a brilliant job in New York City, partying with my friends and feeling truly independent. I hadn't really thought it through. I didn't have a plan, but I was determined to start this next stage of my life in a powerful way. I knew there was something out there for me, even if I didn't know exactly what it was.

I didn't have much, but I packed up all that was important to me, everything I thought I couldn't live without, you know . . . like, *all my stuff.* Even though I was ready to be an adult, I made sure I didn't forget to pack my favorite stuffed animal, Tigger the Tiger. I kissed my dad goodbye. My boyfriend shook his hand and together we got into my loaded up beige Dodge Colt. We were on our way. Get ready, New York City, (erm, Long Island) here I come!

Since it was late when I was dropping my boyfriend off in Brooklyn at his new apartment, I decided to spend the night. I was worn out from the emotional stress of leaving home and the anticipation of what was ahead, not to mention the physical exhaustion of packing up. We were both so tired from the long day, we didn't even think about the risk of leaving my precious stuff in my car overnight. And even if we did, there was the flight of stairs up the stoop of the brownstone to consider. I mean, why I would move all of my bags again just for the seven hours I was going to be there?

What could go wrong?

I locked the car doors, trudged up the steps and went to bed, ready to dream of my fresh start tomorrow.

The next morning, I bounded down the steps ready to finish the journey. But something seemed wrong.

Tigger was on the street.

How did he get there? Wasn't he packed in a bag? The broken glass next to him didn't clue me in on what I was about to realize. When I looked up, reality clobbered me. The car window was smashed.

All of my stuff was gone. Including my last two paychecks carefully placed in my Filofax.

Tigger was all I had left.

My most precious belongings, all the things I needed for my new life were gone. My clothing. My cameras. My box of letters from my besties and boyfriends. My connections to my past and my home and all that was familiar to me. Vanished. *Gone.*

Faced with the suddenly urgent need for basic necessities, I learned that survival didn't include *stuff* (although I was grateful that I still had Tigger). The keepsakes that were stolen ultimately didn't mean much compared to not having clothes.

Once I got past the shock of this experience, I faced unexpected questions:

- Without my stuff, who was I?
- Who do I want to be?
- How do I want to live?
- What do I want to bring into my life?
- What essential things do I need for my life to move forward?

And I needed to get the answers quickly. Without the security and safety net of how I had defined myself, I was living out a speed round of the effects of letting go. Because I had to be clear about what I needed, the new flowed to me easily because there was literally nothing in the way.

The day after I was robbed, I landed a job in a retail clothing store that paid far better than I could have imagined. Within a month, I got a lead on someone who was selling a Nikon F-3, the camera I'd always longed for, which was far better than the two hand-me-down cameras that got me through my school assignments. I still use that camera twenty-eight years later. The things I thought would be hard to attain and take years to afford came into my life easily. Along the way, I discovered what my stuff meant in my life. There was a direct connection between what I owned and my quality of life.

I'm sharing this story because I learned in the deepest way what it means to let go. I know what it's like to no longer have precious belongings I believed I couldn't live without. I understand the questions you will face as you start to let go. It's not easy. You will have a lot of feelings about it. At first, I was inconsolable that I would never read the treasured letters I had carefully saved or wear my favorite high school track sweatshirt again. But even though they were physically missing from my life, my memories of them and *the experience of having them* were still with me.

I was learning how hanging on to my past through objects, and my beliefs about them, could become a trap by setting limitations on who I could or might become. Letting go put me on the path. While I didn't have a choice in letting go of the objects themselves, I had to make the choice to let go of how I believed those objects defined me and my life. By letting these beliefs go, I could see the endless possibilities they were blocking. I discovered I could choose my life in a way I hadn't before. Without this experience, as heartbreaking as it was, I now recognize that my life wouldn't be what it is today.

Letting go taught me that I had the power to transform chaos into calm.

The choice belonged to me.

Just like it belongs to you.

THE CHOICE

That's all you're doing here - making one simple choice: Do you want to live in chaos or calm? As my clients struggle with what feels complicated and intimidating at first, I guide them back to this one choice. I remind them to look at it another way: Are you choosing to make room in your life for who you want to be? Clearing space is the invitation. As my clients let go of the items that feel negative and heavy, they begin to feel and appreciate the items that light them up. Transformation occurs. Chaos, and the fear it creates, will keep giving way to calm as they keep making room for flow. The interesting thing is, once they do let go, they can't remember why they were holding on for so long.

I know expecting and accepting change is difficult. Even if what's familiar drives us crazy, it's still scary to give up the way things have been. We are creatures who seek comfort and *what we know* is always more comfortable. The future is unpredictable, so we hold on desperately to our past because at least we know what it is. Letting go of stuff is also an exercise in letting go of who you were. It allows you to reimagine yourself. Making that choice is an act of permission to keep evolving in ways that may be different from who you always thought you were.

But in order to have that breakthrough, you may experience what feels like a breakdown first.

Don't be scared; I'm right here.

TWO FORMS OF RESISTANCE

You're not going crazy. I promise. This is just our familiar friend the amygdala making sure you are "safe" by trying to keep your ego happy. That old lizard brain wants to keep stomping around in the cave he knows best with his many necessities in his sight. As you start changing your known environment, you might also start to panic and find any means to halt your progress. That's just resistance showing up with perfect timing, like that no-good ex-boyfriend who always knows to call when you're feeling most alone. (Block that number!)

This resistance shows up in two different ways, usually dependent on the object being parted with:

1. **Emotional.** There's no way around it; choosing to let go of stuff is emotionally challenging. You will have a lot of feelings to feel, as you come across things from your childhood, your family, ex-lovers and former jobs. Some of it will make you happy (the science project that earned you second place in the sixth-grade science fair), others may make you want to full-on retreat to bed (the boxes you never unpacked from two moves ago). But remember, not feeling your feelings is what got you here in the first place. No one likes loss, or even the idea of losing things. Feelings about loss suggest hard questions and invite us to examine ourselves more deeply than we are comfortable doing. So, it's understandable you might resist this. That's human. But, go ahead and shed some tears or have a few laughs at those maroon leg warmers from the '80s, and stay connected to your vision of who you are now.

2. **Logical.** This is the extended dance mix of your playlist compiled from previous chapters:

- I spent good money on this.
- I'll break my mother's heart.
- I might need it someday.
- It's in perfectly good condition.
- This is valuable; I'll sell it.

Or your own version of bargaining that you easily fall into. These are great arguments to make. After all, they make perfect sense. They satisfy your ego's need to be right. But as we've taken these arguments apart earlier in this book, don't forget that what's seeming like logic is an attempt to avoid feeling uncomfortable. Stop and breathe for one moment. Remember that you have already learned to see these excuses for what they really are: fears designed to limit your future.

So, yes, those shoes cost two hundred dollars. They looked amazing and matched that dress perfectly. But the night to wear them came and went five years ago. They were (and still are) crippling. The thought of wearing them again is unbearable. However, a voice in your head reminds you that they're so pretty and were so expensive . . . Trust yourself that you can find shoes that are both beautiful and comfortable the next time you have a hot date and are ready to show off your latest dance moves. Why block the energy of a more comfortable and useful pair of shoes? The memory of that evening and how fabulous you looked is still available to you without taking up valuable space. Let someone else have the opportunity to dance in those heels.

Together these forms of resistance hide the *real* underlying anxiety: How will I know I lived without my stuff to prove it? I want to be careful here. I'm not telling you which items you personally need to let go of. Only you can decide that. What I'm pointing to is how often we think we need to justify ourselves by holding up an object and saying or thinking, "I had this experience and here's the thing that proves it". With my clients, I come across a lot of yearbooks, graduation caps, and Econ I & II college textbooks. Whether or not they decide to keep those objects, doesn't change the fact that they still graduated from college. (As far as I know, no one has ever asked for a graduation cap as a form of credentials for a job interview.) Objects only represent the experience through which we have lived and gained knowledge. Whatever you decide about letting go of your stuff, the experience and knowledge remain. No one can ever take that away from you. So maybe that 30-year-old fraternity beer stein that you've glued together more times than you've actually used, can move on while you wax nostalgic about that raging kegger from senior year to your heart's content.

This anxiety is less about letting go of your stuff and more about the passage of time. Ultimately, you're sensing your own mortality. This is a tender spot and it's normal to feel vulnerable here. Going through your belongings, you see how far you've traveled in life, how much you have changed. This recognition is quite poignant and I'm grateful to have witnessed and learned from my clients as they come to appreciate where they once were and where they are now.

While I was working with a woman whose children had moved out years ago, we went through her enormous collection of shoes that had taken over one of her child's empty bedrooms. I had her try on every single pair to see how she felt in them. There was a wistfulness in the air as she chose to part with her higher heeled shoes that she didn't feel safe walking around in anymore. This was a bittersweet moment. It was important to honor her genuine feelings of time passing by. She bravely confronted changes in her body and the changing needs in her home. I invited her to focus on how well she raised her kids and what great adults they've become. Now that the room was cleared, there was space again. We were able to replace the 30-year-old twin mattress with a queen-size one so her son and his spouse could easily stay with her when they wanted to visit. And her edited shoe collection left her feeling confident that she could choose any pair and walk without worry of injury.

Many of us act as though the best years are behind us because we are surrounded by our past. Is this true? I invite you to flip the script here: What if we look at this process as a celebration? Letting go proves our growth. It reminds us that we're not static even if we think we are. We look at children and expect them to grow and change - we do everything we can to encourage that - so let's give ourselves that same gift of freedom as adults. Releasing what we no longer need can be an uncomfortable reminder of aging and loss but, more importantly, it's an invitation to expansion and possibility. We're not alone in this. Everyone faces these same questions.

Thinking back to that terrible morning in Brooklyn when it was just me and Tigger, I certainly have moments when I would love to see those letters my BFF wrote to me in high school. It would be fun to see what she wrote on one of those five-page-loose-leaf-front-and-back-covered-with-blue-ball-point-pen-hearts-and-exclamation-points-folded-perfectly-to-be-passed-discreetly-in-class letters. As you can see, I haven't forgotten them and the excitement to read them as well. What's even better is planning lunch dates with her so we can laugh about our dramatic teenage selves, all the while having new experiences together and creating new memories as we share current and future secret dreams.

I know this isn't possible in every situation. There are connections that feel like they've ended either because of distance, life choices, or death. Often, we believe that hanging on to items that represent that relationship is the only way to hold on to the memory of those who are no longer with us. We believe that letting go of an item means letting go of a treasured person, or the memories of them. As I've watched my clients face this sensitive question, I've noticed that they come to understand that the sadness they encounter is more about the passage of time and the identities they've outgrown and left behind. While I would never want anyone to get rid of *all* of their beloved's mementos, I find that my clients realize that those they've lost are always with them in their hearts and minds, through their memories and stories. And, no matter what they decide to let go of, that person, or that version of themselves, will be with them forever.

Lurking below the surface of these beliefs about memory and connection are the troublesome thoughts like, "Which stuff will represent *me* when I'm gone? Who will hold on to it?" Often this is the lightbulb moment for people. They get quite clear that they don't want to burden those closest to them after they're gone. In fact, this can be all the inspiration they need to declutter. If at first, they're not motivated to do it for themselves, they can do it for their family. Once they start thinking about grieving loved ones having to sort through their most personal possessions, or having them endlessly searching through piles of paper for that one piece with the computer login password so they can shut off the electricity or close-out any accounts, is a powerful motivation.

And it's kind, too.

Both to them and yourself.

This is the pure energy of letting go: generosity.

Letting go is giving the great gift of peace. The only peace you can truly receive is the peace *you* give to yourself.

We're programmed to believe there's going to come a point in life, probably near the end, where we'll be praised or rewarded for everything we held onto. Isn't that a long time to wait? Do you need to keep moving your great grandmother's cast iron pot, which you store in the oven but never use, anytime you want to roast a chicken for the next thirty years? This may seem like a small thing, but it's just one of the hundreds affecting your life every day.

Go ahead. Be generous to yourself. Release the burdens of ownership and responsibility that go along with having too much. Decide for yourself just how much is too much. Wake up to the idea of the fluidity and transient nature of your life. There is no perfection to strive for here. No exact number of items you should own or remove from your life. Surround yourself with the things you love. Forgive yourself for buying those authentic hot pink cowboy boots that never came out of the box and let them walk the life they were meant to live on someone else's feet.

If you can't let go of who you were, you won't have room to grow into who you are meant to become. The peace you've always wanted is waiting for you to make space for it.

HOW

8

DIGGING UP THE PAST

n the first half of this book, you've put your energy and attention on why you have the stuff that you do and why it's impacted your life in ways you haven't understood before. I know these haven't been easy connections to make. You've been brave and patient to do this work. I'm proud of you for staying the course. You've primed your mindset properly to get started on the heavy lifting that lies ahead. Here's the good news: that lifting will be a lot lighter and easier now that you've built a strong inner foundation to make lasting change. You're standing on solid ground now. (And, for all of you eager beavers who skipped ahead and are starting here, good luck! But really, start at the beginning. You'll thank me later. I promise.)

You now understand your shopping habits and emotional ties. You have identified the beliefs and habits that have been keeping you stuck in your clutter. You are a fully tricked out ninja able to face the booby traps in the hallway closet of doom. (Take that, you dusty, old porcelain figurine collection from Great Aunt Tilly!) You'll be able to purge and recycle tall piles of stretched out and torn tee shirts. You'll power lift bags of too-small-acid-washed-jeans into the hands of hipsters who'll wear them. When faced with a flood of unruly paper piles, springing open drawers filled with instruction manuals from 1991, your secret superpowers - the vision you've created and the knowledge of your value - will keep you afloat and steer you to higher ground.

You've got this.

For the rest of this book, I'm going to lay out a plan of action with simple clear steps for you to take. You know why you're living in this mess. Now I'm going to show you the steps to get out of it for good.

Ready?

TAKING STOCK

What do I mean by taking stock? Over the years I've learned that most people don't really know what they own or simply forget what they have. Once they begin this work and literally see what is taking up precious space, they are shocked to discover how much they own. After the surprise fades, they are confronted by their shame. But I'm there to remind them this isn't about judgment, and we keep going. Feeling bad about mistakes won't help here. Again, this is just the block that shows up because they are headed into unknown territory, which is scary. I promise them, and all of you, there will be no public broadcast about your past purchase errors.

It's so much simpler than that: to properly create order you need to know exactly what you own. Seeing and sorting through all of it is the only way to make determinations about what you really need and what you really don't.

MAKING INVENTORY SEXY AGAIN

My first job out of college, the one I got after my car was broken into, was at a discount designer retail store. I dreaded inventory days. Not only was it overwhelming and tedious, but it was also stressful because we had limited time to complete it before the store opened.

I'm not asking you to do that.

You won't be making a list and count of everything you own. Rather, you'll simply be choosing and sorting what you want to keep. You'll see the physical evidence of the many ideas discussed in earlier chapters. By seeing your stuff all laid out in front of you, you'll instantly be able to identify the difference between impulse purchases and essentials. As I mentioned, this will be a long process to get through the first time. It may feel slow as you begin, but that's true for any education. When you start to get impatient, remind yourself you're learning how much of the stuff that comes into your life is temporary or unnecessary. You're figuring out where you are in order to decide where you want to go.

With this valuable information, you can start implementing new behavior that lines up with your beliefs. You'll be inspired to make new choices when you shop. You'll learn to put things back where they belong because now, they have a logical place to go.

IT'S ABOUT TIME

As you get ready to implement the practical steps of clearing space, you're going to need to block off time. Set time in your calendar as you would if you were to meet a friend for brunch or to schedule an important meeting. Please keep in mind the anticipation of the work is the worst part. I know you're going to say "Smith, I don't have enough time to do all of this. I didn't realize how much time it was going to take."

Nice try.

People who say they don't have enough time to get organized stay stuck in a cycle of band-aid-mess-band-aid-mess-band-aid-mess leaving them frustrated and believing they suck. But not you. You're choosing to finally end that cycle. This is where you call in your vision. Don't set yourself up for failure with those past voices in your head saying that you are bad at this. You've made the choice to leave behind the band-aid-mess cycle once and for all. Your choice will make a commitment to your patience as you give up quick fixes. Think about taking a class: you invested time so you could master a topic or skill. Being organized is the same thing. Some of it may come naturally. What feels awkward at first means you're still practicing what you're learning. I promise it will eventually become second nature once you get started. From start to finish, there will be times that will make you want to flee and go make chocolate chip cookies. Or burn down your house. Or burn down your house while making chocolate chip cookies.

This is exactly when you need to keep going.

WHAT ABOUT RESISTANCE?

Many people I've worked with tell me they want to run away as the piles on the floor keep growing. Or they give me their deer-in-the-headlights vacant stare once they're covered in dust-bunnies after clearing out what's been under the bed for ten years. Full of fear, they're not sure they can go on.

But they do.

And you will, too.

As you brush those dust-bunnies off, here are some ways for you to work with any resistance or fear you may experience:

- Practice forgiving yourself for the pain of money poorly spent. Know that you are building awareness during this process.
- Drop any feelings of blame, shame or guilt. Recognize this is only distraction and procrastination trying to edge their way in.
- Don't work alone. Find a friend to work with you (and you can return the favor!), someone who is not afraid to tell you that you never looked good in that outfit.
- In order to create momentum, start with something neutral where you have no emotional attachment, like junk mail.

- As you come across things that pull at your heartstrings or divert you down memory lane - and you will find them in every room - recognize that what feels like a warm bath of old memories is just a form of procrastination. It will keep you stuck. You'll be making a pile of memorabilia throughout the process to revisit later. Set them aside for now.
- Stay grounded in the vision you created. It will keep you bolstered and strong when you feel fear. Re-read the earlier chapters again if needed to see where you might be stuck.
- At this stage, you're only sorting things out in the space to see what you have. It's not about creating order yet. Don't get ahead of yourself. Don't even go down the road of thinking about how these things will be organized. We'll get to that in the next chapters.
- This is only about gathering information. It's an excavation. A study. Stay curious. Be the detective, not the judge. You're looking at the concrete reality of your beliefs and habits that no longer fit or serve you.

If you feel you need a trial run for practice, the easiest place to begin is that one storage space where your stuff goes to die. You know the one. It provides the most out-of-sight, out-of-mind quick relief: the basement, attic, front hall closet, under the bed or in an off-site storage unit. (While you are at it, do the math and see how much you've spent to store the various things you don't use.) It's a goldmine filled with the most obvious items that you can let go and will help build your confidence and momentum. There's nothing stressful or frightening about releasing broken furniture, random old appliances, or crusty cans of paint (please be sure to dispose of these according to your state laws). You'll also be making room for the deep storage needed as you take stock to make your rooms functional.

PREPARATION

What you'll need:

- **Time:** Depending on the size of your home, don't expect to be able to complete this in one day. Give yourself at least four hours, and a maximum of two four-hour sessions with a nice break in between any day you schedule this work. Don't do this spur of the moment or at the end of a long workday. Plan ahead. Bring your fresh brain and energy. If you get tired or overwhelmed, step away, breathe, and refresh yourself.
- **Containers:** bins, bags, boxes. You do not need to purchase these. You have everything you need in your home! For most categories, piles will do.
- **Post-its:** to label your containers and piles. Again, do not purchase these, scrap paper and tape work just as well.
- **Markers:** for the Post-it's and to make any notes.
- **Water:** for necessary hydration!
- **Music:** for inspiration and energy.
- **A friend:** for moral support, help with heavy lifting and possibly regifting.
- **Your objective eye:** and the excitement of a fresh start.

What you don't need:

- **Visual distractions.** Phone goes away. Notifications off. TV off. Computer off. Ship the kids off-site, if you can. Trust me, you *will* look for distractions and excuses, so be prepared!
- **Guilt, shame, and judgment.** Give yourself a break.

Have fun with this! You are sorting in the way *your* brain works, in the way that makes sense to *you*. Some piles will be obvious, like "papers" or "charging cords." Other piles may need a classification based on location, such as "nightstand", which might include your: alarm clock, lip balm, coaster, lamp, framed photo of your pet.

No matter how you decide to label your piles, here's my only rule: YOU ARE NOT ALLOWED TO LABEL A PILE "RANDOM" OR "MISCELLANEOUS." Be creative. Ask yourself which department you would find it in a store.

VERY IMPORTANT THINGS TO NOTE

1. Take any urgent/time-sensitive/daily use/important items (keys/phone/bills/medication, etc.) and put them in one location outside of the room you are working in. Make a note in your calendar or write that location on a Post-it and place it somewhere like the bathroom mirror so you remember where these important objects are.
2. Before tackling your clothing, be sure to do your laundry first before you begin making piles! You need to have every article clean. Don't set yourself up for failure here. You need to see a category in its entirety to have an easy path to success!

GET STARTED

Make a complete list of all the rooms in your home. (This includes entryway, hallways, and pantries that may not technically be rooms but where there is stuff.) Select the room or area that will bring the most relief to you first. This is your choice. But to demonstrate the process, let's start with the bedroom (which has the great side effect of restoring the possibility of proper rest).

Here are the steps to help you see the overall process:

1. Have enough boxes or bags labeled for every room in your home. As you go through your bedroom, you'll place any objects that don't belong in the bedroom in the appropriate box: dishes go in the kitchen box, toiletries in the bathroom box, papers in the office box. Keep asking yourself: Where does this belong? Where do I use this?
   Note: Don't waste time taking these items to the correct location. You'll get sidetracked. Also, you'll be looking for an escape from time to time. Don't do it. Stay in the bedroom.
2. Have garbage and recycling bags at the ready to throw out the obvious trash. Depending on your local recycling laws, you may also need bins for plastic bags/bubble wrap/bubble

mailers and clothing that is too damaged to be donated. H&M and Zara are great resources for these items as they accept clothing donations in any condition as part of their recycling program, even your stretched-out old underwear.

3. Create an area for donations. If the room is too crowded when you begin, put the donation pile outside the bedroom door.

4. Pick one corner of your bedroom. Start here. Going clockwise around your bedroom, pick up each item you come across and start making piles of like-with-like in broad categories: paper, clothing, toys, work stuff. These are quick decisions. Don't overthink it. You are just taking action. It should be very easy to have helpers as you make the piles; that's how broad these categories are. You're not asking the hard questions just yet. Just make piles. It makes no difference where they are in the room.

5. Empty any shopping bags and boxes. Don't assume you know what's in them. (Put the bags and boxes in the recycling pile and grab as you need them for other categories.)

6. After going through the surfaces your bedroom - floor, nightstands, dressers, chair, bed - go through the storage spaces in the room - closets, shelves, cabinets, and drawers - and keep adding to the piles.

As you are putting things into these piles, keep asking yourself these questions:

- What do I use?
- What am I holding on to that I think I might need someday?
- What am I holding on to for the memories attached to it?
- Does this suit me anymore? (This is where your friend comes in.)
- Who can benefit from this? (My personal favorite)

By being curious, you'll be surprised by the discoveries you make about what truly belongs in your space, what triggers shame, and what is actual clutter.

WHAT COMES NEXT?

Now it's time to look at these piles you've created and assess what's there. You may notice small piles that make sense to merge with another pile, for instance: your jewelry + essential oils + journal = top drawer of the dresser pile. Once that's done, take a good look around. There is real information here. Don't miss it. Soak it in. What category is dominating the space? Are there over one hundred books in the bedroom and zero bookshelves?

This is the beginning of discovering not only the actual storage needs for your things but what your habits have created over the years. By seeing the physical reality of your stuff, you'll begin to better understand who you've been in the past in order to make new choices for who you are now. You may have the epiphany that a certain category belongs in a different area of your home even though it's *always* lived in the bedroom just because it's a habit.

During this process, invariably there are seemingly random things that people don't know what to do with, so they throw them all together. I promise, there is either a category or location that makes sense for these items and sometimes, when we can't figure out the category, it's a clear sign to let it go.

Once you've sorted the entire bedroom, take out the trash and recycling. Bring each box you've labeled and put them in the proper rooms. Place the giveaway items in an area by the front door you've designated for all eventual donations. Take a moment and notice how different the room feels already. See how much space you actually do have. Feel the freedom from all the stagnant energy that has been stirred up and released.

Great job! Snack break - a celebratory cookie is in order!

Seriously, set the timer for twenty minutes and go for a walk outside, or take a nap. Refuel and hydrate. You have permission to leave the room and get a change of scenery. Don't give in to the temptation to hop on social media or turn on the tv. This break calls for nurturing, not distractions. You don't want to give resistance an opportunity to creep in.

After your break, you're ready to do some general staging of the sorted piles. Staging simply means assigning temporary locations in the bedroom for these piles so you can find what you need. Once this is done, grab that list you made of the rooms in your home and cross off your bedroom!

Now it's time to move onto the next room on your list.

Repeat the same process, asking the same questions in each room. At the end of your work sessions, when every room has been crossed off of your list, you can continue with Chapter Nine where you'll learn all about proper storage practices.

Wherever you are when you have to stop for the day, you'll want to make a detailed note or voice memo of what you were doing when you left off, especially if it will be a few days before you can get back to this work. Do not rely on your memory!

9

UNDERSTANDING STORAGE

Good for you! You did it!

"**B**ut did what, Smith?" you may be wondering. "Sure, I've created piles of *like-with-like* and I've let go of so much, but when is it going to look like my Insta feed? What do I do now?"

Keep breathing. Trust me, you've taken the biggest step. You've decided what you love, what you use, and what you don't need. You're already stepping into your future, even if that means stepping over and around some temporary piles to get there.

Congratulate yourself.

Really. Look at what you've accomplished so far. It deserves a celebration. You've let go of so much stuff that has been holding you back. Even if it doesn't feel or look like it at this moment, you've created space. I want you to take in the magnitude of work you've done. Look at the donation piles and think about how many people who will benefit from your generosity. Look at the bags of recycling, filled with papers and plastic items that were in the way of the objects you truly need and love. Understand you've completed the hardest part of this journey. Enjoy the view from the summit of the mountain you've climbed.

"But, Smith," you'll ask, "how the heck do I get back down from here?"

Step by step. That's how. Let's go slow. Don't get ahead of yourself or panic about where everything needs to go just yet.

All of those rooms filled with piles are the organized chaos that places you right in the necessary and unavoidable messy middle of creating order. Most of us focus on either "before" or "after." Remember: you're not in the "after" just yet, you're still in between. It's normal to feel more anxious here than when you started. Breathe. It's all good, I promise. This is the time to remember your vision. Keep calling it back. Have faith that, with any transformation, there's that moment where it feels impossibly hard before it gets easier. There's no way around it.

This is the point where your amygdala is going to say "Danger, Will Robinson!" trying to return to the safety of the familiar chaos it knows. It will be looking for an escape, tempting you to run away and go buy cases of pretty bins to simply shove those piles away and out of sight. Please don't. You're not ready yet. You don't have all the pertinent information you need for that step; buying organizational products at this stage is a setup for failure.

Trust me, and trust yourself, that you can stay with this discomfort just a bit longer.

We're going to slow down for a moment, but only just a moment.

Before you can transform those piles into order, you must first understand the existing storage in your home. By knowing how your closets, shelves, and drawers function and the potential they hold, you'll discover which storage options accommodate which items best and how to modify those options when necessary. This is the last bit of crucial information you'll need before you put things away.

CLOSETS

Closets are a big deal.

There is a rumor that Thomas Jefferson invented the hanger and I joke that closets are still built with his wardrobe in mind: a single hanging bar and a shelf above. Most believe this is what a closet should be and then make do. We make do until the closets are bursting at the seams and can't take anymore. Closets are the secret weapon to guaranteed success in taking back control. They offer more unlimited possibilities and solutions for creative storage than you might imagine. Because of their potential, I've found closets to be the best place to concentrate our resources, even more so than containers. And closets have the added bonus of keeping your Renaissance Fair tavern wench costume wrinkle-free and out of sight when your curious ten-year-old nephew comes to visit.

Whether we own or rent our home, there are ways of working with and restructuring the guts of a closet that can fit any budget. Let's start with a simple solution: by adding a second rod in a closet which is thirty-six inches wide, it can now hold seventy-two inches of clothing. Voila! Storage space has instantly doubled. A solution can be temporary and adjustable. Let's say you will only be in this apartment for a year. Rather than build a custom solution, you can do something as simple and effective as moving a dresser into a closet. If you need a more permanent solution, as your budget allows, there are many excellent custom-designed systems available.

Here's a great example and a common problem to tackle:

Almost everyone has that one closet, you know the one with the single useless rod and three empty wire hangers dangling on it. It holds the vacuum, some memorabilia and anything else you can toss on top. There's a four-foot pile which makes finding the holiday ornaments an all-day project because you have to remove all of the contents of the closet to get at them. Imagine how easy this would be with shelves. By simply adding shelving, you can now see the contents of the closet and access anything you need easily. You stop the cycle of overbuying items you've forgotten about because they are at the bottom of the pile since you can now easily see what you have.

Now that you know the potential of your closet, here's where completing your inventory really pays off. You know how much you have and you can easily determine how much space you need to store it in a way that makes sense to you.

I can't stress enough how important it is to understand exactly how much a closet can hold versus what you expect it to hold. Just because you want everything to fit in one closet, doesn't mean it will. Some of my best learning about this came from my work with The Container Store. I was surprised when customers expected me to make their eighty pairs of shoes magically fit into their existing closet by adding a shelf or two. I thought it was common sense that only an eighth of them would fit. Once I created a design that mapped out how many shelves would be required to store their lovely shoes, they began to understand that three-quarters of their clothing would have to be removed to allow enough space for their shoes. They began to make the connection between the actual volume of their things and the physical size of their closets. They knew they had more choices to make and began to consider what else might be possible. Usually, by touring the rest of their home and teaching them to think beyond the one closet, they found other places in their home to keep their shoes that made sense for them.

To help you maximize the volume of storage in your closets, here are some questions to consider:

- Will my items comfortably fit into the closet as is?
- Can I maximize the space by adding shelves? How many will I need?

- Where else makes sense for my items to be stored that I haven't considered yet?
- Do I need a closet professional to help me create a more functional space?

You'll be able to easily answer these questions because you have equipped yourself with real information: I have ten suits. I have twenty blouses. Information is power. It's not what we think we have, it's what we *know* we have.

Some reminders:

1. Sounds obvious but think about what kind of closet it really is and what's best to be stored in it. (Does it really make sense to store your vacuum cleaner with your coats?) Keep questioning: What would be better? Where does it make sense for these items to live?
2. Stay realistic about what will fit in a closet. Measure!
3. Use this as an opportunity to further edit your stuff. It's another chance to re-evaluate and let go of the extraneous. Think of these spaces as boundaries. If the limits are exceeded, it's time to eliminate.
4. Keep returning to your vision and purpose. When you feel there are too many decisions to make, resist the urge to "solve" the problem by jamming things back in your closets. This only starts the cycle of clutter all over again.

SHELVES AND CABINETS

At the risk of repeating myself, like closets, shelves and cabinets (any kind of shelving enclosed by doors) have wonderful possibilities. But shelves and cabinets also have the greatest number of pitfalls. I'm pointing them out here so you can avoid these traps as you work with storing things on or in them.

Shelves, whether open or enclosed, create the greatest opportunity to attract clutter. Have you heard the phrase "nature abhors a vacuum"? Well, shelves are a natural vacuum. They're an easy reach and usually, there's some empty space on them. It's tempting to drop the mail on a shelf as you pass by or to leave your tangled headphones that you will deal with "later" simply because it's a convenient surface (and a convenient place to forget about them, too). Open shelving attracts clutter like a magnet. It also attracts a lot of dust and grease. Therefore you really need to think through where you are organizing what, and how you need it to function. You already have the tools to not get snagged here.

The main benefit of shelving is how it allows for easy access to the items you need, whether in your kitchen, bathroom or office, and the ability to put something back in its proper home. And since you've worked so hard to select the items which you love and value and want to enjoy, open shelving offers you the chance to display and enjoy these items fully. Think about giving your shelves some breathing room and rhythm by placing framed photos and plants in and around your books. Besides creating visual interest, it makes it easier to see what's on the shelves.

Bins, large and small, are a natural complement for keeping your shelves ordered. There are many attractive bins available now. I do recommend experimenting first with plastic take-out containers, glasses, and shoeboxes. These can help you determine the right sizes and shapes you need and to see if containers are really the correct solution for these spaces. This also gives you the opportunity to test whether clear or opaque containers work best for you. Remember: the right-sized bin on a shelf will make a world of difference, not only for the clear space it creates in your bathroom but also for the peace it restores to your marriage since you will no longer have the frustration of hearing your mother-in-law say, "It's surprising you have so many expensive hair styling products when your hair is always a mess."

Three reminders:

1. Once you have determined their proper size and shape, label your bins, so you never have to waste time searching a shelf for what you need.
2. Any shelf deeper than 18 inches will make it difficult to see what's stored on the back end of it, let alone reach what's there. Here's the essential place to use properly labeled bins, boxes, or add a pull-out drawer to access the back.
3. Do not buy containers larger than the size of a case of wine, especially for any shelf overhead or that requires a ladder. Always be sure you can handle the size and weight of an item, box, or bin on any shelf. Proper storage doesn't ask you to be a hero.

DRAWERS

Like closets and cabinets, drawers offer many hidden options for storage. Because drawers come in so many different sizes and shapes, our approach to working with them will, again, vary according to your specific needs. Here are some simple tips and questions to consider how to get the most out of, and into, your drawer space:

- **Always remember like goes with like.**
  - Pens, pencils, and supplies (paper clips, staples, etc.) for the office become a drawer.
  - In the kitchen, eating utensils are separated from cooking utensils and if space permits, we separate out the prep tools (can opener, peeler) as well.

- **Drawer size matters.**
  - A deeper drawer isn't always better. Think about the volume of the items you're storing. Large bulky items like sweatshirts or pots and pans are best in a large drawer. Socks and underwear or jewelry are great in small drawers.

- o If you have only large drawers to work with, now's the time to experiment with stacking bins and drawer dividers to create more functional storage.

- **Keep it all within easy reach.**
  - o Which hand do you use? Being right-handed or left-handed can make a big difference in where you decide things should live, especially in a home office or kitchen.
  - o Start to take notice of where and how you reach for what you need while you're doing a task.
  - o Remember, too, as drawers go down, whether in a dresser or built-in, place all lesser-used items towards the bottom.

- **Slow down and experiment first.**
  - o Please don't go out and buy a bunch of dividers and boxes first and then try to fit things in. Experiment at home with things like small boxes you have on hand. See how things go or don't go, together and if their placement works with how you work.
  - o The smaller the collection of objects is, the smaller the footprint of its container will be. For example, thumbtacks are best stored in a shallow small gift box or tin rather than a mason jar.
  - o Measure first (and twice). Resist the urge to buy the wrong sized containers only because they're cute. And only buy the containers after you've tested with ones you have on hand.
  - o Remember this is a work in progress. Go out and get the dividers and containers as you need them. It took me several years to realize that, even though my husband and I have the same size drawers for our clothing, my drawers were always a disaster while his remained orderly. They were a mess because my small tops were sliding all over the place every time I opened a drawer. By containing my clothing with bins and dividers, my drawers instantly became tidy.

- **Vow to quit the habit of shoving things out of sight into a drawer.**
    - ○ Now that you've done the hard work, isn't it just easier to put things back where they belong? Remind yourself that you know where everything goes and that you don't have to fall back on old habits.

Throughout this book, I've only made one rule for you: don't label your piles "miscellaneous" or "random". You will be tested against this rule as you bargain with yourself to keep your junk drawer. This is my biggest non-negotiable: NO JUNK DRAWERS! You don't need one. You know what belongs in that drawer already: rubber bands, small tools, twist ties, keys, birthday candles. With the proper drawer dividers and your items sorted, it won't be a thirty-minute project to untangle the one rubber band you need. Not only will this order save you time, but it also eliminates unnecessary frustration that can impact the rest of your day.

If you can't find what you need in under a minute, you're on a treasure hunt.

While sorting out their junk drawers, my clients have discovered long "lost" valuable items such as jewelry and eyeglasses which have repeatedly been replaced because they couldn't be found. This is when they discover that by stashing things away without understanding how their storage works, they have only been clearing off surfaces to give an illusion of order. And, in fact, they've only been hiding things from themselves. Their three pair of scratched eyeglasses prove that they've succeeded.

1 0

CREATING ORDER

E ven though it's taken nine chapters to get here, you've arrived. Finally, it's time to put things away and bring order to your home.

Order is a scary word for most people. It suggests confinement, discipline, hard work, grimly eating your vegetables or a cold perfection from which no one can ever deviate. Ever! Order feels like a test you can never pass or the looming drill sergeant who'll demand you give them fifty pushups the second you step out of line.

That's not me. (Well, it could be me if you keep your junk drawer or have piles labeled "miscellaneous" . . . don't make me come over there!)

And that's not what we've been talking about.

Before you begin to put things away, I want to offer some ways of thinking about organizing so you take the next steps with knowledge, confidence, and clarity. Check-in with your vision. Keep moving forward connected to your understanding of what being orderly is and isn't, and what order means to you.

ORDER ISN'T...

Order is not a one size fits all solution. Instead, order grows out of creating solutions that are as individual as your DNA. By studying your successes and mishaps of your routines, you're now able to design your home so it functions like a well-oiled machine that works specifically for you and your family. Order transforms the stress in your home into a much-needed source of peace away from the stress from life outside of it.

Becoming organized is not a personal punishment, a lifelong penalty you're sentenced to because there's something wrong with you, or because your closet is bursting with ten years of old clothes. No one is coming over to write you up with a ticket or charge you a fine.

ORDER IS...

Most of us forget that creating order is simply arranging things so we know where they are and where we are in relationship to them. Think of the different kinds of order we rely on every day: alphabetical order, numerical order, chronological order, size order, seasonal order, directional order, and color order. We couldn't navigate our day without them. We take them for granted never fully appreciating the ease with which they hold our lives together, both as individuals and within communities.

Imagine walking into the grocery store after a long workday to pick up a few ingredients for dinner. What if the aisles were filled randomly and you had to hunt and peck your way through the store? There you are, rooting through cereal and cake mix boxes trying to find a box of pasta, or digging through cartons of milk and bags of cotton balls looking for a package of ground beef that's out of your reach underneath a family pack of paper towels.

You're tired. You're hungry. You just want to get your things and go home. But you can't because you can't find anything.

And the store is filled with other frustrated people on the same search. It's mayhem. You figure you'll make do with whatever you've unearthed and are ready to get the hell out of there, starving and exhausted. But there is no line. Just a mass of people waving their credit cards and cash hoping to be the next one to flee this nightmare, all dreading the search for their cars in the chaos of the parking lot which has no clearly marked spaces, lanes, or traffic lights.

Who would want to face this every day just to get dinner?

No one would accept that.

So why do so many accept this way of aimlessly living in their homes?

We're so used to thinking of order as an authoritarian command imposed on us from above, which our inner teenager instinctively resists and wants to rebel against (Hello, amygdala! I see you in that disguise!). We lose sight of the basic fact that order exists only to simplify our lives, not make them more difficult.

Really. That's it. Order is a way to make your life easier.

Let your inner goth teenager rage if needed, but, remember: You're the boss. The order that you create is your own and it serves you.

So, go ahead. Get to it!

GETTING STARTED

Now that you have sorted your belongings into categories and understand how your storage works, it's time to decide where it makes the most sense for these items to live. Some categories, like "tools" (screws, nails, hammers, wrenches, duct tape) may make sense to live together in a cabinet or closet. Other broad categories, like books, may be divided into different areas of the home (cookbooks can live on a shelf in the kitchen, self-help books in the bedroom, etc.). Experiment. Learn the limitations of your spaces and the volume they will comfortably hold. (By *comfortable* I mean, you can look inside a drawer or cabinet and not have to dig around or take things out to find what you are looking for.)

Stay curious and ask questions as you assign new homes to your piles based on their ultimate purpose. Be honest about what fits and what doesn't. Above all, be patient with this process. It's okay to be thoughtful and take your time here. Don't get hung up here on making this perfect. The homes where you assign your categories aren't permanent. Both will evolve with you over time. What makes sense now may not make sense three years from now and that's normal.

Set up your bedroom in a way that's your idea of a sanctuary for rest. Set up your kitchen, so you're free to nourish yourself and your family with ease. Set up your living or family space, so you are comfortable relaxing together. Set up your entryway, so you can arrive and depart effortlessly. Keep asking yourself "How would this be better?" Be bold and play with options. Imagine better storage systems. Swap furniture from other rooms. If necessary, treat yourself to a new piece of furniture. And, if you can't find a home for something, make my favorite choice - eliminate more stuff!

Along the way, pay attention to how you move through your space. There's valuable information here so you can make easy and efficient decisions about where things belong. For instance, track the tasks you do every day. Remember back in Chapter Six when I asked my client to walk me through how they make their morning coffee. It seemed simple enough, right? The coffee maker is on the counter. Mugs in a cabinet. Coffee and filters are in the pantry. They were surprised when I pointed out how many extra steps they were taking every day to make this one cup of coffee. It may not seem like a big deal, but when you add up each small daily routine, you can see how many obstacles you're inadvertently throwing in your own way, and how all those extra minutes start to accumulate.

One way around this is to think about the daily tasks you execute in each room. When you're in your kitchen, trying to decide where things belong, start by noticing the things you must do every day. Make a list of them. Set up your cabinets in those rooms so each day-to-day job has its own individual location. Make a coffee station in the cabinet above the coffee maker which includes everything you need to brew your coffee: cups, grounds, filters, and sweeteners. Use the same approach for smoothie stations. Do this in your other rooms as well for categories like toiletries, clothing, or work materials.

As you make these stations, also think about what needs to be in easy reach. For most of us, "easy reach" is the general range between shoulder height to knee height as you face your shelves, cabinets, and drawers. You don't want to pull out and then climb a step stool every day to grab your protein powder or crouch down to the bottom shelf to get your blender, as part of making your morning smoothie. "Easy reach" also means considering how much an object weighs. This will be an important consideration for any items that are left once you finish setting up areas for daily tasks and your storage spaces begin to fill up. Lesser-used lightweight items can go up on higher shelves. Things like heavy pots and appliances which are used less often can go on lower shelves or into deeper storage.

Some of you are probably wondering, "Smith, what if I am not the only one using the space? Whose brain gets to decide where things live?" I've noticed nine times out of ten most household members have little to say about these decisions. But you don't want to assume that's going to be the case for everyone either. Ask questions. Notice that "easy reach" means something different for your tall husband. Observe that your kids naturally tend to leave their backpacks in the same place that's different than the place you've assigned. Collaborate. Compromise. Make decisions together when, and if, you can. But I'm also giving you permission, without judgment, if you need to decide that the snack drawer is kid height, so you don't have to stop preparing dinner to get them a treat each time they're hungry. And remind yourself that none of these solutions are irrevocable.

THE MAGIC QUESTION

Now that you're establishing what order is for you and how that order will take physical shape in your home, here's the magic question to ask yourself as you start to put things away: **How often do I use this?**

This question often cuts through uncertainty you may have about where things might go. By studying what you use on a daily basis, you've already seen how this question simplifies what you need around you and where it belongs. As you make your way through the rest of your inventory, keep asking this magic question. Your answer will break down into one of three ways:

- **Everyday:** anything you use more than three times a week
  - Utensils
  - Small appliances
  - Active office files
  - Toiletries

- **Short-term:** monthly
  - Extra bedding
  - Sporting equipment
  - Hobby items like art supplies, sewing, crafts
  - Hardware and home improvement items

- **Long-term:** once a year/deep storage
  - Holiday decor
  - Seasonal clothing
  - Memorabilia
  - Tax returns

Once you know how often you need to access certain things, you will intuitively know where they belong so you can maximize your storage areas and bring ease into your life.

Let's look at a common item like a rolling pin. It's awkward to store and can eat up a lot of storage space. By analyzing how often you actually use that rolling pin, you'll quickly figure it out where it should live. If you bake fruit pies weekly in the summertime, it makes sense to keep the rolling pin in an easily accessible area like the top utensil drawer. If you use it a few times each year, it could live in a lower drawer along with things like muffin tins and pot lids. If you're a once-a-year holiday baker, it's best to pack it up at the end of the season with the holiday cookie cutters in your deeper storage area.

I'm going to repeat myself with a few reminders:

1. **Slow down:** it's okay to take your time here.
2. **Stay curious and aware:** remember the magic question.
3. **Crawl before you walk:** don't buy containers until you've tested with what you have on hand first. (Shoeboxes, take-out containers, etc.)
4. **Have fun and experiment:** it's a game of trial and error. Remember, there isn't one perfect way.

To show you how all of these steps and ideas came together, I'm going to share how I worked with them in my home. My husband and I had a problem every time we needed to leave the house together: He was in my way. I was in his way. Our coat closet was small with one hanging bar. It was set between the banister and the front door. There was no way for either of us to grab our coat, put it on, and leave the house if the other one was trying to do the same thing. It was a logjam. To get around this, or just to get out of the house, coats were left on the banister and things had a way of piling up and getting misplaced.

One day I had enough and came to my senses. It was time for a fix. Since I was tired of the daily struggle, I needed to find more space for our coats. But where? In the end, this resulted in a surprising transformation of my home office. Here's what happened. I decided to restructure my office closet to make room for my coats so the front closet could solely hold my husband's coats. That way we'd both have a clear path to come and go, and peace would be restored to our home in the bargain.

Simple enough.

My office closet was full of shelves. How was I going to make room for those coats? And then I realized that this was an opportunity for me to re-envision the way I used my office because, when we moved in several years earlier, I hadn't started this business yet. My needs had changed dramatically but my office space had not. In fact, my office hadn't kept up with the changes in my life at all. I didn't notice this until I faced my closet full of shelves filled with crap I wasn't sure I still needed or not.

I began to empty the closet, taking everything off the shelves. I created my piles of like with like and started making discoveries: I had three staplers! I had fifteen sketchpads! Time to purge. Once I saw everything in the piles, I was able to make new decisions. I always said I wanted to draw and paint more. Wouldn't it be great to have my art supplies right at hand?

But there was a problem. My desk didn't have any drawers. When we first moved in, I decided that I wanted a large workspace for creative projects. I had a six-foot white countertop made by a local kitchen and bath company which was placed on two desk supports. Even though the supports had two shelves, which could be accessed from the front or the side, they were mostly useless. They were great for my cats to play or sleep in, but terrible for storage. I learned the hard way that a desk without drawers, no matter how good it looks in a furniture website or showroom, is as useful as a blender without a lid.

Now was the perfect time to create the desk I needed which would support my work. Since I was working at home more frequently and spending too much time sitting, I knew I wanted a standing desk. The big lightbulb moment occurred when I realized I could replace the supports with two customized banks of drawer units at counter height. This would give me a ton of storage outside of the closet and keep everything organized, contained, and not on top of my desk.

As simple as this all sounds, it only became so because I could see the piles of categories and had mapped out the storage spaces. Then I asked the magic question: How often do I use this? First, I considered what I rarely needed: my slide projector, slides, all of my negatives and prints, my camera equipment, and boxes of old letters. They could all go into deep storage. Since my ceilings are high, I installed shelves at the top of my closet to hold these items, with a bar underneath to hang my coats. There was still room underneath the coats to hold two more shelves for boots, handbags, and hats and scarves.

First problem solved!

Now that I had desk drawers, I decided one column of drawers would be dedicated to office/work stuff: my files, office supplies, and the tools I needed when I'm on-site with clients. The other column was designated for play - paints, crafts, tools, and paper.

But there was a challenge.

I now had nine drawers of various sizes and more than nine piles remaining.

I'm going to give you a tip that will change your life when you face a similar problem as you create order. Take the drawers out and bring them to the piles. When the drawers are in place in a unit, you can only open one at a time which makes it harder to see how much potential storage space you have. I like the vantage point of seeing the drawers all at once. This gives an accurate and instant understanding of what each drawer can hold. By seeing where one drawer is tight, and another still has more room, you can experiment with combining categories and creating an individual sense of order.

When I had to face those extra piles, I began to play with what could live together based on what individual drawers could contain. Some categories were very small and would require dividers so they wouldn't roll around the drawer making a mess and getting damaged. Since dividers are meant for an entire drawer, and the category only took up one-quarter of a drawer, I really looked at what other items of similar size might fit in the remaining space. The answer made for an odd pairing: Beauty and Electronics - lots of lip gloss, hair ties, nail polish, travel-sized perfume, digital camera, phone and camera chargers, extra headphones, mini tripod. These small items fit together perfectly in the divider trays that I purchased. As it turned out, they are also the miscellaneous items that I often use at my desk or need to throw in my bag before leaving the house. There was an intuitive logic behind this grouping. Having a designated space in the drawer makes it easy to put them away rather than leaving them laying on my desk or throwing them in a random drawer - you already know how I feel about that!

Once I matched the drawers to the piles, I labeled each one. Even though I am the only one using them, it's good to have a reminder of where things are so I don't have to open and search every drawer when I have a timely task to accomplish.

When there is a collection of items forming on my desk, like now with six bottles of supplements and essential oils, or when I dig through a drawer, I know it's time to rejigger the way I'm currently storing things. Rather than feeling like something is wrong, I'm excited when I make changes to these drawers because it means I am growing.

That small physical change in my environment is an expression of a bigger change afoot. Think back to how we described order at the start of this chapter: *Order is knowing where things are and where you are in relationship to them.* That's all it is - a way of staying oriented. Order is a tool you create to navigate the best way forward.

For you.

By seeing where you are, you can see what your next step might be.

As you create order in your home, you're striking a balance between what you invite into it - with a newfound extremely critical eye - and what you will release. This balance will always be shifting because your life is always shifting. But you will be able to stay grounded because you know where you are. You have a sense of the terrain ahead.

This is your new truth.

And that's all you need.

11

BUMPS ALONG THE WAY

Six weeks have passed since finishing the work through Chapter Ten. With a newfound sense of pride, you're enjoying ease and peace in your home. You're sailing through your day. And then there's that day you can't find your charging cord. That "perfect" place you found to keep it isn't so "perfect" when you have to go up and down the stairs when you get home to charge your phone, which you forget to do when you leave your phone on the kitchen counter while making dinner.

Frustration starts to take hold when you realize your phone has died midway through following a recipe in the cloud. Wasn't the point of finding the "perfect" storage place meant to avoid these kinds of problems?

Back away from the ledge!

This doesn't mean anything is wrong. You haven't failed. All that hard work you did wasn't in vain.

In fact, it's good news! Behind that frustration is an awareness that the system you created isn't quite right, which means you've become highly attuned to how you need to function in your space.

You have become a researcher, beta-testing all the systems you created. It's inevitable that there will be bugs and glitches along the way. The only way to find this out is by living with the order you've created and observing whether or not it aligns with how you actually live in your home. If you discover a problem, you do not need to hammer out the ideal solution in the exact moment when you realize something isn't working as you hoped. There may not be an immediate answer. Set your judgment aside and ask a few questions. The lightbulb moment will occur when you least expect it. The most important things are that your awareness has grown and you're comfortable knowing that there are no absolute permanent solutions.

I'm so proud of you.

As you step further into the refining process, here are some questions you can ask as you run into snags. They will help you as you make tweaks:

- What's not working?
- What would be better?
- Does this make sense?
- Is this functional?
- Is this beautiful?
- Are the systems I've created working together?

Here are some examples of how you'll keep making small adjustments as you continually enhance the order you've created so it works best for you.

You're making breakfast one morning. You notice you're annoyed by how challenging it is for you to get the frying pan you need. When you first organized the kitchen, you were thrilled that every single pot and pan nested inside each other in a drawer. They were finally in one place and fit together perfectly. But this solution isn't functional for daily use. You're still having to move things to reach what you need.

How could you know this without having the experience of testing it out?

Now's the time to gently ask yourself "What would be better?"

A few days later, while making your morning coffee, you look up and see an open space to hang a pot rack. Eureka! It's the right answer for your needs. And, with this one move, you've freed up a drawer which has given you and your kitchen room to grow.

Let's say you decided to put your books in the bookcase by the desk in your office. After a couple of months, you realize you haven't reached for a single book once. But your desk is covered with growing piles of things required for a big, new project which you need to access daily. In order to have space to work at your desk, you're constantly having to shuffle files and supplies. There's just no place to put anything.

As you look up where your walls and ceiling meet, you realize that you could have shelves installed around the perimeter of your office for those books. This opens up space for bins inside the bookcase to hold your files and keep your workspace clear. If the bookcase with bins looks ugly to you, another option may be to replace it with a filing cabinet or drawer unit. You've become confident knowing that there are always other possibilities.

Most of the time, a simple fix is all you need.

While getting a client settled after her move, we decided to store her family's tote and travel bags on the shelf above their coats in the closet. They all fit perfectly in this space. I followed up with her several weeks later and she told me how frustrated she was about the coat closet. She felt that it was always a mess even though we thought we had found the right places for everything. The source of the mess was easy to find. Whenever she reached for one tote bag, most of the other bags would fall down. Because she was often in a hurry, the bags remained on the floor inviting the rest of her family to leave their bags on the floor too. Clutter was looming. Even though it all seemed great on move-in day, it hadn't been tested against the daily routines of four humans. The bags were in the right place, but the solution wasn't functional yet.

We needed a way to contain the bags while keeping each one within easy reach. We talked about adding bins but quickly realized that taking an overhead bin full of bags down each time she needed just one required too much effort. Since we were on the right track, we kept asking "What would be better?". The thought of a tray or something with a lipped edge came to mind. I went to The Container Store with my measurements in hand. As soon as I saw the under-bed storage baskets, I got excited. They were only four inches tall, and as my luck would have it, two of these fit exactly side-by-side on the shelf. Not only were they functional, but the woven baskets were beautiful and coordinated with her style as well.

Nine times out of ten, making these adjustments are this simple.

IT'S NOT ALL ABOUT YOU. (This time.)

But there may be times, as you flow through your space when it feels like something is off. Skilled beta-tester that you are, you've ruled out the cause being your stuff, because you've already released so much. You know your systems are working well because you've kept refining them. This is a big clue that the issue is not about your stuff. Most likely, it lies in the physical structure of your home, a seemingly unalterable detail to which you became resigned. You believed for a long time that's just the way your home is. But now that you're open and curious, and enjoying how functional your home has become, you're starting to wonder if that "unalterable" detail can be changed after all.

I've seen this happen in my own life.

When we moved into our current apartment thirteen years ago, I knew my kitchen was going to be a challenge. It was small, narrow and a third of the size of our previous one. Spoiled by the vast space we used to have - an eat-in kitchen with two walk-in pantries! - I wasn't quite sure how to make this new kitchen work for me.

But we tried our best, making the most of what we had. Downstairs, we had an odd-shaped hallway that was quite wider than usual. We installed six four-inch deep shelves that gave us forty feet of vertical storage for all of our pantry items. As I kept refining and felt that everything was where it belonged; something was still off. The kitchen itself remained hard to navigate.

It was a logistical nightmare whenever my husband and I and I tried to cook in the kitchen at the same time. If we left the door open for the cats, it wasn't possible to open the dishwasher or oven door. Whenever we had a party, it was a challenge to get to the sink or open the refrigerator door, let alone get out to the deck. It was really puzzling because everything was where it belonged. It's not like we were stepping over piles on the floor.

Even though the solution wasn't obvious to us, and as we continued to curse the people who designed the kitchen, we knew somehow that it could be better.

Our second winter was much colder and snowier than the first. During one large snowstorm, I walked into the kitchen and stepped in a cold puddle. I looked up and noticed that there was a huge gap between the top of the door and the door jamb. The snow was coming inside.

We called our building's management company and they said they would replace the door. Since they said we could choose whichever style we wanted, I asked for a French door so we could let more light into the kitchen.

Once the old door was off its hinges, the solution to our struggle was right in front of my face. The swing of the door went into the kitchen rather than opening onto the deck. It was one of those structural details that we just accepted because that was the way it was. Seeing how much clearance there was without the door provided me with a great idea. Here was our opportunity to make this small space more functional.

This was truly the magic fix!

The threshold for this doorway was a foot deep on the outside of the door. I asked if we could install the door on the outside of the threshold and have it open out. This was quite easy for them to do. The repairmen were surprised by how much better it made the space. We all were. After we shared a laugh about not noticing the obvious, I realized the power of asking questions. I was curious about why so many of us are reluctant to do so.

I used to expect skilled laborers to always know what was best. And they do. But, most of the time, they approach their work with a specific assignment in mind like "install the new door." They don't show up ready to suggest alternative ways to maximize the functionality of a space. After this experience, I realized how often in the past I'd allowed the authority of someone else's expertise to muzzle my curiosity, when, in the end, I'm only curious about what could be better. Now that I'm unafraid to use my voice, I usually learn one of three things:

1. An expert has a better answer which they're excited to share.
2. There is a structural reason why that specific change or request won't work (which means asking if there's another way to get to a similar result)
3. Someone needs to be pushed (gently and kindly) to do the work.

This happened with a client.

A new client contacted me to help organize her kitchen after her recent renovation. I knew she had just spent a lot of money and sacrificed not being home for a few months, in order to create a beautiful and functional kitchen. But it didn't work as she had hoped. She showed me the cabinet where she was keeping her children's art supplies, the stuff that will very quickly ruin walls, carpet, and sofa, and which required supervision: paint, glue, scissors. As I watched her open this cabinet, I saw the problem immediately.

This upper cabinet was on a wall that was perpendicular to a peninsula counter that divided the kitchen from the living area. Like most cabinets, the doors opened from the center to the outside. The only way to see what was in the cabinet was to stand directly in front of it. But, to do so in her kitchen, meant standing at the end of the eight-foot peninsula . . . eight feet away from the cabinet itself. Or by taking a seat on top of the counter. If you stood on either side of the counter near the cabinet, the opened door would be in your face blocking your view and access to the shelves inside. You would have to reach under the cabinet door, grope around, and hope for the best. (Not the best approach when reaching for things that could become an instant bomb of liquid mess if dropped.) These cabinet doors were a breeding ground for clutter and would be impossible to keep organized.

But, because I am no longer shy about asking questions in my quest to find a way to make a space more useful, I hit upon an unconventional solution.

What if we changed the swing of these cabinet doors so that, instead of opening from the center to outside, we moved the hinges to the center support and the doors now opened from the center to the inside? Rather than pulling the doors open and *away* from each other, the doors open *towards* each other, so they met in the center of the cabinet. This way, no matter which side of the counter she stood on, she could look directly into the shelves and access what she needed easily.

Both the client and the contractor were doubtful. (More than doubtful, but that didn't slow me down.) At first, my client said she didn't think it was possible. When I asked why she replied, ". . .

because . . . that's . . . not . . . normal?" I asked the contractor what he thought, and he said it wasn't a good idea. When I asked him why he thought so, he replied that the door handles would have to be moved and that doing so would leave visible holes.

Still smiling, I asked one more question: to move the hinges to the center, couldn't we just swap the doors instead so the handles wouldn't have to be moved?

Crickets.

I took one more deep breath.

I explained that if we took the right door and put it on the left side, and took the left door and put it on the right side, the hinges and handles would be in the correct location without having to remove them or leave unsightly holes.

One hour later, as I was leaving, I saw that the doors were already switched. No muss, no fuss.

And this solved the problem!

I may have been as happy as the homeowner to see this immediate transformation.

I want to encourage you to start looking around your home for these kinds of obstructions which are hiding in plain sight. Again, now that you can finally see your home free of clutter, experiment. Perhaps you'll find an additional three feet of wall space for more storage after you switch the closet door from opening into that closet to opening out into the hallway instead. You'll be surprised by how much space you can keep creating.

LIVING IN POSSIBILITY

Back in the mid-nineties, I was a commercial photography agent trying to make sure my photographers always had work. They would regularly ask me when their portfolios would be complete. I would always have to stay on them to create new work. Each time I asked for new portfolio pieces, I had to be ready to answer the same exasperated question: "Is my portfolio ever going to be done?" My reply was always the same and delivered with a big smile: It will be done when you're dead.

Each opportunity for a job required presenting the work that best showcased their ability to carry out that job. If the client needed us to shoot an apple for their ad, and my still life photographer had a portfolio with images of watches, furniture, toys, an orange, and a pear, the fruit imagery would be moved to the front so the client can see something in line with what they were shooting.

The photographers who were consistently employed understood that the key to their success was their ability to adapt to circumstances and keep their work fresh. They knew their portfolios were a continual work in progress and they enjoyed seeing the evolution of their style in the process. They were confident it was as close to right as they could get it for today.

And tomorrow's idea of right might mean something different because something else will be needed. There is always another possibility.

This is where you are: adapting to what's best for you in your home right now.

Like the photographer who needs to curate how she expresses her abilities based on the work she's being asked to do, you'll need to adjust your home in thoughtful and simple ways depending upon the work you're asking it to do. New situations will require new answers. Even though you've established a terrific baseline of order with your stuff, your life circumstances will shift. Here are some examples of when your home might need to catch up:

- Your son starts playing hockey and now there's a trail of smelly gear throughout the entryway.
- Your daughter goes off to college.
- Your new trainer has you on six supplements and the bottles are cluttering up your kitchen counter and you are forgetting to take them.
- The season changes: you find yourself with nothing to wear.

Rather than feeling defeated when these situations come up, you need to remember all that you've learned and that you already have the skills to nip any pre-clutter problems in the bud. As you anticipate or notice changes, adapting solutions becomes effortless.

You've reached the freedom that comes from riding change like a wave, surfing on the energy of what's possible.

12

BACK TO KINDERGARTEN

What now?

Is there anything else to do?

You've learned to let go. You've cleared space and made it beautiful. The transformation has happened. You've even celebrated.

As you walk around your home enjoying how great it feels to know where everything lives and have space to breathe, you're now thinking, "I'm done, right?"

You *are* done. (Basically.) The heavy lifting is finished. (It really is.)

The only remaining question is, "How do I keep this going?"

The answer is so simple; you won't even believe me. It involves my patented system I like to call *Put Your Shit Away Every Day.*

That's it.

Honestly. That's all you have to do. You know where everything goes now. There's nothing left to figure out. It's a simple execution. Put things back where they belong. That's all you need to do. No muss, no fuss.

If you need a bit more structure, it looks like this:

- Make your bed daily.
- Do your dishes daily.
- Set a weekly laundry schedule (which includes folding and putting your clothes away).
- Schedule a 30-minute weekly straightening session (as you listen to your favorite podcast).
- Plan a 15-minute weekly paper purge to keep up with the mail.

It really is that easy. It doesn't even require that much of your time.

But I understand for some of us that kind of maintenance instills deep resistance. It feels like being told what to do or being burdened with yet another task when life has you overburdened already. It's the perfect invitation for our old friend, the inner brat, to pop up annoyed that someone has told her, one time too many, to clean up her room. *I don't want to!* just seems to be the natural human response.

And, look, there will be days when life gets in the way and you don't want to make your bed. Old habits and beliefs will kick in insisting you don't know what to do or that it takes *so long* to make the bed even though it only takes three minutes. You have the ability and tools to snap yourself out of it. The difference, after going through the process I've laid out in this book, is that you now understand why there is a place for everything. When disorder hits - and it will - it's only a five-minute fix back to normal. This takes a little while to fully master because your brain is still wired to anticipate a lot of hard work, much like my younger self felt about doing the dishes.

Allow yourself to be a kindergartener again. Put things back where they belong. Easy-peasy. And give yourself a gold star from me while you're at it.

Here are three ways to think about maintaining order when your resistance digs its heels in and start to feel like you don't want to:

1. **Big Picture: Love Yourself.** Self-care has become trendy; it's easy to dismiss as selfish indulgences like frequent bubble baths or mani-pedis. By doing this work, you've invited flow into your life and embraced the potentiality it brings. You've chosen to be responsible for yourself and your home. Living in chaos felt chaotic. You've chosen something else. With that in mind, and remembering what chaos feels like, I invite you to keep making those same choices. I want to remind you that you are worthy of this kind of care. You deserve a home that nurtures and restores you.

2. **Small Picture: Take Care of Yourself.** Keeping order is like brushing your teeth. Making the bed (and much of maintenance) is as simple and easy as that. It's just something you do every day because that's what you need to do to take care of yourself. I know this doesn't sound inspiring or sexy. Even so, it's a good reason. Flossing your teeth every day can add years to your life. Imagine the difference living without added stress in your home makes. Taking an extra few minutes to put things away in the home you created for them is worth much more than the few minutes less you may be on social media. And it will make you feel better too. If you keep up with your stuff by monitoring the breakdowns, you'll be in good shape for a long time to come.

3. **Pay Attention.** Since you've started to actively pay attention to what's coming into your home, you might have noticed that your shopping habits have shifted. While in a store or browsing online, you've probably caught yourself asking the questions "Where will this live? Do I really need this?" But there will be those days when you're mad at your sister and stressed out at work, and the tempting call of the end-of-season clearance rack beckons. Look at those Jimmy Choo shoes, they're seventy-five percent off! Take two seconds

and pay attention here. Breathe. Ask yourself: "Where will I wear these? Do I really need them? Will they just become clutter?" With this single moment of attention, the urge will pass. Be proud of yourself for staying present and choosing calm over chaos. Honor that choice.

Yes, there will be times when your inner stubborn toddler kicks and screams, "But I don't want to!" It's going to happen. Be prepared for that moment. Allow it. Know that any tantrum will ultimately wear itself out. You can't have ice cream for dinner every night. (Well, you can, but there's a price to pay one way or another.)

The same way you've anticipated that there will be an occasional tantrum, I want you to be prepared for some potential traps which surface when life happens, pitfalls I've seen time and time again. Once you're aware of them, you'll know how to work with them so you can regain your balance quickly. (Don't forget: Your life is growing and changing. Expect your space and systems to keep adapting.)

- **Pitfall 1: You don't recognize when a new circumstance needs a new system.** That's fine. Here are some clues that you're in this situation: You can't find what you need. Something is always in your way. Piles are forming. Simple tasks become frustrating. This always means a current system isn't working well and should be changed.

  Example: You've found the *perfect* exercise class and you're finally working out four days a week. AMAZING! But now there's suddenly a backup of laundry. The daily search for your favorite sports bra has you running late for work. The solution isn't to stop working out. You need to readjust your laundry schedule and create a drawer specifically for your gym clothes. To keep your new positive habit going, the mantra here is a familiar one: Ask how would this be better? Stay curious and remember there is no perfection.

- **Pitfall 2: Life happens. Temporary disruption to your regular maintenance schedule occurs.** These kinds of events are perfect triggers to bring back old habits. They invite feelings of overwhelm which could easily sabotage all of your hard work. You will probably default back to believing "I don't have enough time for all of this."

  Example: Your workload unexpectedly changes, and you have to travel more than usual. Mail starts to pile up. The refrigerator needs to be cleaned out. The exhaustion of not sleeping in your own bed catches up with you. Seizing upon what looks and feels like a disaster, your amygdala will convince you that you've messed up, you're bad, and it's all too much to fix. The hard work you did was for nothing so it's best to leave it alone.

  Example: Your child is sick in bed for a week. This plays havoc with your schedules at work and at home. You have to prepare different meals for the sick child as well for the rest of your family. There are germs to disinfect and more laundry to do. Stressed out, you feel like you just want to give up because, just for that moment, you feel like you don't even know where to begin.

  Take a deep breath here (or several).

  Be gentle with yourself and remember that you've already solved these problems. You know what to do. Everything has a home now. The choice to not fall back into chaos is easy - put something away. Even if it's just one thing. This single step can help create the momentum to remind you that you know what to do. Taking an action is always the answer but you may need to take a nap first.

- **Pitfall 3: Other people will magically know my systems.**
Since you were the one who was most likely responsible for creating the new sense of order in your home, it's tempting (and perfectly natural) to think everyone else in your home will understand what made intuitive sense to you and why. With systems now in place, you expect them to "get it" and get on board with maintaining these systems. But things still end up in the "wrong" place or go missing. You feel frustrated that the help you need, whether from your husband, or kids, or cleaning lady isn't happening, or sometimes they seem to be making things worse. You tried, but, in the end, you believe you're on your own, and your home will always be in chaos.

Example: To keep up with your laundry schedule, you have two hampers for dirty clothes in your bedroom closet, one for you, and one for your husband, so you can gather the laundry quickly. But your husband keeps leaving his dirty clothes in a pile on the bathroom floor because that's where he gets undressed before his nightly shower. His hamper stays empty. He's not messing with you on purpose. Or is he? You're starting to wonder why he won't work with you and why he's making your life such a living hell (also maybe you're just a wee bit cranky that day).

Example: Now that you're no longer embarrassed by the state of your home, you've decided to bring a cleaning lady in weekly to help you keep things neat and tidy. One evening, after she's cleaned, you can't find the remote controls for your TV and all you want to do is watch Season 5 of *Outlander*. They should be in the basket on the coffee table but they're nowhere to be seen. Did she steal them? No, that's crazy . . . is it crazy? Where are they?!!! After a frustrating search, you discover them in the side pocket of your reclining chair, a side pocket you completely forgot about. In your mind, you accuse her of not doing her job properly and wonder why no one understands what is so obvious to you. You realize your trust issues may also need to be addressed.

What both of these examples have in common is that it may feel like everyone is clueless and you have to do it all yourself if you want it done correctly. While it seems that way, what it really means is that they need to be taught the method behind your madness. No one else can create a system for you, or intuitively understand your current system, unless they've had the opportunity to walk through your thought process.

It doesn't mean they're not doing their job or trying to drive you nuts. I'm sure they're trying their best, but they don't have all of the information they need. You haven't patiently explained your system fully or completely, which you have to do, as well as be prepared for everything not working for everyone immediately. It's an opportunity to be responsible for your choices. Communicating your expectations, and being open to discussing other solutions, is the best way to continue living in order.

Collaboration, along with kind communication, is the fastest way to create harmony in your home. You're not the Order Police, citing people for violations; instead, you're curious about why something isn't working. You're always on the lookout for workable evolving solutions, rather than feeling burdened or judged as the family nag.

Usually, it's just a matter of talking and letting go of the feeling that you're being bossy by explaining why an item lives where it does. There is a big difference between being clear about why something is organized the way it is and asking for support in maintaining that order versus demanding that everything be your way. But many of us feel like asking for what we need is the same thing as being unreasonable.

Don't be afraid to take ten minutes to talk to your family or the cleaning lady. Find out what they think. Answer the questions they have. Be open to their ideas. Stay curious. Listen. There's no reason to be scared. People are happy to help when they truly understand what you're working towards. And they will enjoy living in a home that's full of good energy and peace and not jammed with stuff.

- **Pitfall 4: A family member won't get on board.** If you remember the description of the person at the beginning of Chapter One, there is a good chance that you'll have a family member who is perfectly happy living with clutter. Suddenly your life has turned into a daily argument with them about putting their stuff away. This fills you with resentment. You're ready to call it quits.

  Example: You spent a weekend helping your teenage daughter declutter, purge and organize her room. A week later, it looks like a bomb went off. How could she not follow the systems you both just created together? After a bad day at work, you fly off the handle and tell her she's grounded if she can't keep her room tidy.

  With kids, the bottom line is it's your house, your rules. However, if peace and ease are the goals of this process, think about where you can compromise or what you can let go of. My advice here is to negotiate and collaborate. Set clear boundaries. Decide as a family which areas of your home are allowed to be messy and which aren't. Don't let the perfect be the enemy of the good. If the way to keep the entryway clear and passable is by having your son throw his backpack and coat on the floor of his room (which you don't have to go into and to which you can shut the door), that's fine. Together you've decided that his mess stays in his room. The important thing is that all of the things you need to get out the door for work are where you need them to be and are always accessible. Have compassion and accept that some people are wired to be comfortable with clutter. They don't see it. And screaming at them won't make them see it either. Have some empathy. Stay in your own lane. The best you can do is be an example. (You may also want to consider meditating more.)

MOVING FORWARD

By now you've seen and felt how these small, daily, weekly and monthly tasks can keep your home in a state of ease and flow. They've become a source that enriches your life - something that benefits your mind, body and soul. Perhaps you didn't realize that's what you've been doing here all along. You've adopted a practice or ritual like meditation or taking up yoga. That's how I like to think about being organized. It's a practice. In order to reap the benefits, you make time for it. By staying committed to small actions, such as making the bed every day, you build up healthy habits rooted in self-respect and care. Your dedication to the simple tasks of simply putting things away is the key to your ongoing freedom. Keeping your word to yourself is one of the best things you can do. Keeping your word to yourself is one of the best ways of loving yourself.

At the risk of contradicting myself, my best advice here is to not take it all so seriously.

You can have fun with this.

Think of the energy you want in your home and conjure those feelings as you tidy up. It doesn't have to be a grudge match. If it feels like one, go deeper. What is really bothering you? Journal about it, meditate on it, keep asking yourself, what is this attitude really about? You can always make a new choice. You can decide to feel empowered by keeping your space in order rather than kicking and screaming and doing it because you HAVE to.

Be the example of how you want your family to feel about putting stuff away. The attitude you have when doing the upkeep is contagious. Can it be easy, effortless and fun? Or at least not a source of martyrdom? If you're furious when you put your kids' toys away, what are you teaching them? What if you showed them how caring for their stuff is a way of caring for themselves, and that living in a home with others requires collaboration and communication? Wouldn't that be something? Think of what a gift that would be for their futures. (And, just to keep it real, maybe you'll make it seem like so much fun that they'll start to put things away on their own.)

The answers to living our most beautiful lives are inside of us.

We just have to be brave enough to listen to them. And then follow where they lead.

So, yes, there will be days when you forget to put something away, or a pile of clothes starts to form. Take a deep breath. Be kind to yourself. You've done the hard part. Your eyes have been opened. Ask yourself: How do I feel when my space is clear?

Pick yourself - and the clothes! - back up.

Remember the secret I told you on the first page of this book? Being organized is the *path*, not the destination.

That's all you need to know.

13

STAYING ON THE PATH

You've finished this book. You've finished the work in your home. You're definitely on the way forward. You might also be wondering, "What's next? Where to now?"

That's a great place to be.

It means you've traveled. One part of the journey is complete.

Take a moment and observe where you are. Admire it. Notice that you are able to see where you are because the stuff that was previously blocking your view is gone. Think back to where you started. Looking back, I know you've surprised yourself. You did something you didn't quite believe was possible.

It turns out it *was* possible after all. You made the decision to take that one step. Then the next. And the next one.

You kept going.

Well, that's what I want you to do now: Keep going.

While your specific destination may look a little different from mine, I believe we're all going in the same direction - a life where we're filled up rather than depleted and weighed down.

Doesn't it feel better to travel lighter?

My hope in writing this book and sharing the knowledge I've gained over the years is grounded in my belief that owning less allows all of us to have more. Not more stuff. But more peace. More experience. More adventure. More connection. More love.

Who doesn't want more of that?

That may seem like a lot to get out of doing the dishes and making the bed and knowing where the things in your home go, but I believe that's how it works. I *know* that's how it works! I see it all of the time.

As people let go of the stuff that's been holding them back, they discover how much clear space they have not only in their homes but in their hearts as well.

So, keep going!

Yes, there will be plenty of times when stuff starts to accumulate, or you can't find things, or it feels like the most unimaginable inconvenience in the world to hang up your clothes. But remember, that feeling of inconvenience will pass. It's not real. It doesn't mean *anything* unless *you* make it mean *something*. It's only a dip in the road; the spot where the way forward doesn't seem clear.

Stop a moment. Breathe. Take a look around. Remember how far you've come. Feel how good it feels to travel light.

And keep going.

If your self-belief falters a bit, I'm going to share with you my beliefs to help you along the way. We're all on the path together. No one is alone. Every step taken is a step forward. As we take them together, supporting each other along the way, we will create a better environment, not just for ourselves, but for life on earth.

So, here goes:

- I believe the path to freedom occurs by being extremely selective about what we allow into our homes.

- I believe that if we make our home environment beautiful, inviting and comforting, it will aid our well-being and should be viewed as a true form of self-care.

- I believe that if we take the time to get to know who we are now and where we want to go in our lives, it's easy to let go of what's not serving us any longer.

- I believe that true happiness only comes from knowing, loving and accepting yourself, not by acquiring more stuff.

- I believe in you.

ACKNOWLEDGMENTS

The amount of support I have received from the moment I decided to write this book is unlike anything I have felt in my entire life. Offering my gratitude on this page feels insignificant compared to what I have received.

First, my deepest thanks to my clients who have invited me into their homes and trusted me and my amazing team with all that is precious to them. By sharing your wishes, giving me challenges to solve, and witnessing your "A-ha" moments fills me with great joy. I'm so grateful that we have come into each other's lives.

The Container Store, thank you for giving me the opportunity to serve your customers over the past six years. This was the best research and education I could have asked for.

Chantelle Adams and The Courage Collective, thank you for making me believe I could write a book and that what I had to say was important. You mean the world to me.

Peter M. Krask, Thank God I told you I was writing a book. Your enthusiasm was infectious and necessary as you dragged me kicking and screaming to the end. Not a chance this book would have seen the light of day without you. Can't wait to see what's next for us! Love you!

Tonia Misvaer, your never-ending guidance on all things beautiful and legal-ish are priceless. I adore you, Candy Jack.

Jocelynn Banfield and Eunice Malick, the brilliant readers of my shitty first draft who encouraged me to keep going and get it right. I hope I did. So much love for you both xoxoxo

My family and friends, I love you. Thank you for your patience and for understanding my absence.

For the incredible people listed below, your existence was necessary and appreciated for this book to come into creation and I'll never forget it:

Lil Girl, Big Boi, Mom, Dad, Patrick Smith, Ross Banfield, Courtney Banfield, Erinn McMahon, Julie Strong, Julia Bernadsky, Nitzan Fridman, Daniel Bobby Tuttle, Carline Pierre, Stephanie Venezian, Theta Healing NYC, Laura Pena, Jenny Powers, Carissa Reininger, JR Mahon, Elena Brower, Shane Inman, Todd Kaloudis, Amy Watson, Deb Friedman, Naomi Pabst, TJ Chernick, Phyllis Mehalakes, Jennifer Sparks, Carey Watson, Erica Roizen Belsky, Becky Linot, Scott Mason, Donald "Monty" Montgomery, Florin Helf, Becky Linot, Lucy Sweeney, Fiena, Jae Raux, Emma Brewster, Sophie Everard, Sabrina Sagoo, Georgia Herbert, Jackie Archis, Adera Angelucci, Ryan Smith, Elisabeth White, Jennifer Racioppi, Julian DeVoe, Soul Camp, Richelle Fredson, Denis O'Dwyer, Brendan Burke, Betty Loos, Rachel Schwartz, Tamara Vanlint, Dolores Storness-Bliss, Steph Rudnick, Maria McClung, Jonathan Kaplan, Sarah Dey and the entire Cheer Me On Facebook group.

And to The Universe, thank you for sending these words through me.